Charles M. Whipple is Professor of Psychology at Central State University, Edmond, Oklahoma. Dick Whittle is Associate Professor of Psychology at Central State University

THE COMPATIBILITY TEST

THE COMPATIBILITY TEST

How to Choose the Right Partner And Make Your Marriage A Success

CHARLES M. WHIPPLE, JR.

DICK WHITTLE

PRENTICE-HALL, INC., Englewood Cliffs, New Jersey

Library of Congress Cataloging in Publication Data

Whipple, Charles M
The compatibility test.

(A Spectrum Book)
Bibliography: p.
1. Marriage. 2. Interpersonal relations.
3. Marriage compatibility tests. I. Whittle, Dick, joint author. II. Title.
HQ734.W55 301.42 75-33010

ISBN 0-13-154005-X
0-13-154013-0 (p)

A Spectrum Book

10 9 8 7 6 5 4 3 2 1

Printed in the United States of America

Prentice-Hall International, Inc., *London*
Prentice-Hall of Australia Pty. Limited, *Sydney*
Prentice-Hall of Canada, Ltd., *Toronto*
Prentice-Hall of India Private Limited, *New Delhi*
Prentice-Hall of Japan, Inc., *Tokyo*
Prentice-Hall of South-East Asia Private Limited, *Singapore*

Contents

THE TEST

COMPATIBILITY—TWO

COMPATIBILITY—THREE

THE COMPATIBILITY TEST

1

Are You Compatible?

Days may come and days may go
of brighter, sweeter gleam
But nothing's half so sweet in life
as love's young dream.

Two important choices an individual will make in life are the choice of a mate and the choice of a career. The success of each will affect the satisfaction of the other. "What do you do?" is almost the first question we ask of a stranger, whether man or woman.

Likewise, when applying for a job, an inevitable question is, "Are you married?" We recognize that a person often brings his or her problems to the job and that maladjustment at home can lessen efficiency.

In our affluent society, both men and women seem to be turning from career toward family relations for greater life satisfactions. Recent studies have shown that the "expected source of greatest life satisfaction" for men was around 65 per cent from family relations and 30 per cent from career, whereas with women it was approximately 80 per cent from family relations and a little over 10 per cent from career. These and other similar studies indicate that the interpersonal relationship between mates is the most important factor in life and the source of the greatest happiness or misery.

An important fact presented throughout the pages of this book is that if a marriage is to last, it must be approached carefully, for such a relationship is all-embracing. It will inevitably involve the total personality of both partners in face-to-face contact. Through such intimate contact of body and personality, people develop strong positive feelings. Responsiveness, commitment, and generosity dominate the relationship, and these we so often interpret as love.

Millions of dollars have been spent by public and private organizations to discover how you can have a better chance of a happy marriage. Several thousand research projects have been engaged in by psychologists, sociologists, psychiatrists and research organizations to find answers to what makes a good marriage. We will give you the results of some five hundred such projects in this book.

Studies of thousands of marriages in which both participants have said, "Our marriage is successful and happy; I'd marry the same spouse again," and at least as many which have crashed on the rocks of the divorce court, have been studied. The conclusion is that almost all marital failures can be traced to certain basic causes. This does not mean that if these could be corrected all marriages would be happy and successful, but that they would have a good chance of being adjusted so that the wife and husband could have an acceptable life together.

The old story book ending, "they lived happily ever after" is an impossible fantasy. Neither in marriage nor while single is a person going to be happy every day. Happiness is a picnic, forgetting the ants. Happiness is a lazy summer day, forgetting that the breeze blew hair into your face. Happiness is a baby's laughter, forgetting the wet diaper. Happiness is a beautiful woman, forgetting the mole on her cheek and the wart on her hand.

Because of this, it is important that you know before the minister says, "I now pronounce you man and wife," that you have picked the right mate and that you are the right mate. There are too many problems and stresses in marriage without chancing the impossible situation of being incompatible.

Marriages break up even when the two love each other, when they are conscientiously trying to make a success of it, though they be deeply religious, regardless of the fact that there may be no money shortage, and when they like the same things. Their friends do not know what happened any more than the mates themselves. Both wives and husbands have cried out in their agony and anguish, "Why, oh why did this happen?"

You see mismated people all about you. Certainly, you do not want to become another couple with a troubled marriage like some among your acquaintances.

WHY THIS BOOK?

We do not know of any book on measuring the compatibilities in marriage. It is long overdue. Although many firmly believe that love is enough and will not tolerate any objection to their "wishful thinking" conviction, we hope that those who have tasted the fruits of matrimony and found them bitter will be more eager for help. In working with those who have gone through a divorce or two, we have found that they are anxious to pick another mate and are serious about how to select the right person.

There are also many couples—some investigators say sixty-five percent of all who are married—who are having problems. The first step in their solution is to correctly identify those problems. This is possible with the Compatibility Test and the information given in these chapters. For many problems, this book will suggest solutions. If one can not resolve his own problems with this material, he is urged to seek professional help from among the clinical psychologists, psychiatrists and marriage counsellors available in the community. Ministers, rabbis and priests are also doing commendable work in this area.

WHO SHOULD WRITE SUCH A BOOK?

In truth the most sagacious man of our age should have touched his pen to these pages; one who has the deepest comprehension of sociology, psychology, psychiatry, anthropology and ethnology; one who with empathetic understanding of the myriad problems of husbands and wives and who could be as prolific with answers as a Dorothy Dix or an Ann Landers and yet have the love and patience of a saint. For twenty-five years we have waited in vain for such a person to come forward with this treatise, but he has not appeared.

During this time, our information was slowly collected, assorted, revised, until the authors felt they should wait no longer. Thousands of tests have been administered, probing the deepest crevices of that mysterious thing which has been called the "human mind."

Perhaps the most revealing result of such work has been the conclusion that most marriage problems are brought into the marriage by the participants; they do not occur after the ceremony. If this is true, then the problems and conflicts are present on the day the couple agree to be married. If one is very smart and knowledgable he should be able to unearth these traits and deal with them before they cause misery. It is also apparent that if these ingrained characteristics are not dealt with, the possessor will carry them from one marriage to another, leaving behind the wreckage of what should have been satisfying and happy homes.

Loving involves a wide circle of relationships. It includes relationships with parents and children, relatives, friends and neighbors, and others. It implies a bond with and concern for all people. Some persons seem to relate well to those in the innermost circle. Conversely, others appear unable to establish and maintain intimate relationships—particularly toward the spouse. Obviously, the most effective individuals are those who have the capacity to relate well in every circle of environment, in the home and on the job.

Compatibility is an absolute essential to family success. Without it, even as a couple stands before the altar, they are headed for a marriage failure. Two incompatible people may remain married for years, but just living in the same house is not a marriage. Some are held together by their hatred for one another and the pleasure they get from sadistically torturing their mates. This is not marriage, but the fruits of incompatibility. As the poet Giles told us over a hundred years ago, "There is no earthly happiness exceeding that of a reciprocal satisfaction in the conjugal state."

Suitability for one's career and compatibility with co-workers are also essential to family success. Unhappiness on the job will carry over into the home and vice versa. They co-mingle and intermix to such an extent as to be almost inseparable.

Naturally, two people who are in love with each other believe that their choice is based upon only individual motives and will lead to personal happiness. This belief, indeed, this absolute conviction is an illusion which is based on a trick of Nature. For Nature can delude the man and woman who are in love that their welfare, their desires, and their happiness will be served by this choice, while Nature herself really only works in the interest of propagation, when she allows the choice in love to occur between them. It is not those individuals who are personally suited for each other who exercise mutual erotic attraction toward each other, but those whose qualities in regard to propagation complement each other. Nature thus serves the interests of the species at the cost of individual happiness and deludes the individual into believing he is following his own interests in his love choice. But here, too, the illusion may be short and the repentance long, unless a compatible selection is made.

People often make business decisions only after mature consideration and then act accordingly. But in choosing a mate, they may not think the choice through at all—not because love forces them to act without thinking, but simply because they do not recognize the importance of such a choice on their own future or its effect upon their children. For the choice of a mate is the important choice, indeed, generally, the most important act of our entire lives. This is because the happiness or unhappiness of domestic life, which is dominated by the marital relationship, is reflected in everything one does. This cannot be too strongly impressed on the person who has yet to make this choice.

There are many who believe that two people when they marry cannot be truly in love. Love takes a "lot of living together" for it to come into being. As Molière said, "more than is believed, love is often the fruit of marriage," not a prelude.

There are three compatibilities. We call them compatibility-one, two and three. *Compatibility-One* is the central, the deep-seated, the more permanent. This is the goodness of fit between the partners' intrinsic characteristics. Without this goodness of fit, two people have little chance of achieving true happiness.

The most extreme incompatibilities show up immediately. In one-third of all of the marriages which eventually end in divorce, these extreme incompatibilities make their fate apparent immediately. This is true even though many of these couples do not actually break up until later in life—sometimes many years later. Those who have the most serious incompatibilities experience a crack-up first; those with somewhat less serious ones break up later; and those with little incompatibilities may stay married indefinitely, but are not necessarily happy, unless they can reconcile these incompatibilities. But how can they reconcile them unless they discover them first? To help find and reconcile them is the purpose of this book and Test.

Compatibility-Two includes the background factors which have been found necessary for "conjugal bliss." We refer to such things as differences in age, education, religion, family background, etc. These can often be adjusted to, compensated for or changed, sometimes by the individuals themselves and at other times with professional help.

Compatibility-Three is growth compatibility. During the marriage, two people grow and adjust to each other through "give and take," by compromising and learning to understand the likes and dislikes of each other. There is also a degree of maturity attained, especially in first marriages. Such growth may require a long time—years. If a couple is aware of this, it should make them more tolerant of the "growing pains" and willing to endure, instead of breaking up.

The purpose of this book is to assist those contemplating marriage, or looking for a mate, to measure Compatibility-One, to better understand self and thus know what characteristics to look for in a mate, and then to test the "intended" to determine if the two can find happiness in marriage. The statement of many young people, "But I love him (or her) and that's all that matters," is childish and immature. That is *not* all that matters. The man and woman who are now bitterly fighting in a divorce court, bringing such cruel charges against each other, and who, even worse, are using their own children to punish each other, were just as much in love when they went to the altar. But love wasn't enough.

Other purposes of this book are to make you aware of Compatibility-Two and Compatibility-Three. Suggestions will be given to help you adjust to those things for which you can adjust, to describe and give some solutions for problems in these areas. This is not to say that unless you have all of the compatibilities, you will be unable to avoid heartache and divorce. There are compatibilities which can be changed, others that can be sublimated or compensated for.

Psychologists who use aptitude tests to fit men and women into suitable careers and jobs have learned that just finding the "right" career does not guarantee success. It only makes it possible. But the person who is ideally suited to the job may fail simply because he does not work at it. So it is with marriage compatibilities. An ideally suited couple may refuse to face the realities of life or to accept their responsibilities as adults and drift into marital disaster. But there are some marriages that seem doomed to failure from the very start. A high percentage of divorces could be prevented by compatibility matching, more careful selection of mates, a better understanding of each other and premarital instruction or study. However some marriages are so destined to failure that no amount of effort by the couple or by professionals can save them. These are the people who should discover the facts before taking the final step, and choose another mate.

Many social scientists are fatalistic about this question. They point to the deep-seated, irrational factors that plague unhappy marriages and to the way divorce infects some families from generation to generation. Human personality is largely shaped in childhood, they tell us, and character defects are likely to stay with a person the rest of his life. There is some truth in this statement, but one *can* better his chances of a successful marriage by choosing the right partner, knowing how to treat the chosen one, taking the trouble to do so year after year, making the compromises and the give and take which is necessary to succeed in marriage.

Divorce is usually a painful, soul-shattering experience, even when the two despise each other and want to be separated. But, even though they were disappointed in their marriage, they usually are not opposed to finding another mate, unless there are religious taboos. Contrary to popular thinking, men are just as anxious for another marriage as women. Women tell of being proposed to on the very first date with a divorced man. Most people feel that a "happy marriage" is their right, perhaps part of the right to "the pursuit of happiness" guaranteed by our Constitution. If they did not find it in the first attempt, they hope to in the next. Surveys show that in the United States, three-fourths of all divorced men remarry and two-thirds of the women. And more would gladly go to the altar if they had the opportunity. Seemingly, at any age, bachelors and spinsters are less likely to marry, while divorced men and women are most likely. For some reason widows and widowers are less likely to remarry than the divorced. Perhaps it is because humans are inclined to forget the imperfections of the dead and remember only their good points; thus, they have more trouble finding another mate who will measure up to the remembered perfection. Children do not seem to be an obstacle to remarriage. Almost as high a percentage of those with children remarry as those without them. Even women with four or five little ones find mates almost as readily.

The average interval of time between divorce and remarriage of women is slightly over two and a half years. Among the above "middle economic class" divorcees, the most frequent cause of divorce is "finding another marriage prospect who seems to better fit the needs and wants" of the individual. One concludes that the divorced have a better chance of another marriage than the widowed or never marrieds and that it will be soon. At all ages over 21, divorced women have a better chance of marriage than the single ones. But their chances do materially decrease after age 45.

Of all marriages, over one-third end in divorce; of first marriages about one-fourth, and about twice as many second marriages end in the divorce court as do 75 percent of the third and fourth marriages. A logical conclusion is that Americans do get a second chance for a satisfactory marriage, but after that, the chances are almost all against it.

Professionals who work with marriage problems feel that just as there are accident prone individuals, there are also "divorce prone" people. Some have so many personal problems they are fit to live with no one. Others may not even try to remarry or may not be able to find a partner who will chance it with them. Of those who do remarry, these "marriage misfits" make up a growing proportion of the successive marriages—a third, fourth or fifth.

A reason for the publication of this Test is because of the lessening chance of success of the third and later marriages. It is to help men and women make their first or second marriage the success they expect when they say, "I do." It is prepared mainly for three persons. First, the one who has never been married, but wants to be. Of this group of people, it is aimed at the ones who, seeing marriage failures all about them, realize that "it can happen to me." These are the ones who have learned from the experience of others that marital success must be based on something more than, "I love him (or her)." Secondly, it was prepared for the divorced or widowed individual who wants to find more happiness in the next marriage than in the previous one. With life so short and a second chance likely to be the last, the second marriage deserves a more careful approach, more use of the head, and not so much dependence on the heart or emotions. Follow the advice of William Penn, the Quaker colonist: "Never marry except for love;

but see that thou lovest what is lovely." And the caution of Austin O'Malley, "You cannot weld cake dough to cast iron." You cannot successfully mate an incompatible couple—such as the following:

> Joe and I seem to fuss all of the time. Before marriage we would have a fight, stay away from each other for a few days and then make up. It was so much fun making up. He was so sweet, apologetic and loving. I suspected that some of the fights were just for the fun of making up. I just knew we would stop fighting after we were married. But the fights haven't stopped. At first, we would pout and not speak for a few days. Then Joe started walking out. The first two or three times he went home to his parents and stayed a couple of days. Now he leaves more often, but goes somewhere else; I don't know where.

No two persons are completely compatible when they marry. This is the reason for Compatibility-Three, the growth compatibility. Indeed, the growth compatibility can and should begin before marriage. But it alone is not enough. The doubts which some couples have may in themselves be incompatibilities. This uncertainty often predicts a broken engagement, or if they marry, a divorce. To say the very least, it is a good sign that the couple is not yet ready for marriage.

It is the *central* characteristics, which we call Compatibility-One, into which this book delves most thoroughly. These are the characteristics which were developed early in life and have become a part of the personality of the individual, or those which were brought into the world at birth from the stream of life itself, or those whose origins are unknown. Social scientists themselves do not agree on the source of these ingrained traits.

> As Dr. Knopf looked through the microscope at a field of living sperm, he called his assistant's attention to their varied behavior. "Notice the one in the lower right quadrant that is flipping around from one piece of debris to another. Seems nervous, excited and full of energy; reminds me of that little red-headed freshman in Lab. 1. And look at that slow over-sized one right in the center. Seems so lazy he can hardly move along; acts like that big hunk of a boy who sits on the front row in the second period class. The one who falls asleep so often."
>
> "That's right," answered the assistant. "And look at the one in the left center. Seems to be waddling along just like Professor Jones in chemistry. Do you suppose, Dr. Knopf, that the same personality they seem to have here would be theirs if they were born?"
>
> Dr. Knopf shook his head in wonderment. "The answer to that question awaits until we can select a few sperm with different behavior

patterns and use them to fertilize human eggs and allow them to be born. It will be an interesting and revealing experiment, but it will probably be several years before it can be set up. The laws, you know."

Scientists are not at all sure of how much of what is called personality is affected or caused by the make-up of the body's anatomy and physiology. There are wide variations with respect to nerve endings and nerve patterns. The close relationship between the nervous system, the emotions and personality is recognized.

Certain of these central traits are more likely to be due to such physical differences in the nervous systems, the glandular make-up and secretions and bodily conformities than sociologists and psychologists have imagined. Even Dr. Knopf may have been at least partly right. But regardless of where they originated—from the physique, from early training or the cultural and environmental background—several of these have been found to be characteristics which should be matched with those in an intended mate. With some of them, if one of the two is high, the other should be also. With others, the opposite is true. But since so few marriage prospects know how high or low they are in these most important traits, the only way to match themselves with a "love partner" is to undergo testing and measurement.

Marriage tests are designed to measure those traits which have been found to be critical in the selection of a mate, but they are only designed to be used with "normals." There are a number of things they will not reveal, at least unless they are carefully interpreted by a well trained psychologist. For instance, the tests in this book will not spot all alcoholics, drug addicts, psychopathologies, the sadist, the potential murderer, or the man or woman who will not work. In the chapter "Freud and Love," tips are given on how to discover many of these.

Of course, authorities themselves disagree on how many factors and which factors would be included in Compatibility-One. But they also disagree on nearly everything else. The qualities used in this test are those which have been found in over twenty-five years of marriage counseling and clinical practice to be the most useful in such work by the authors. The ones used in Compatibility-One and this Test are: heterosexual need, intellectual and educational level, dominance or decisiveness, liking for people, emotional stability and energy.

Loving, though critically important, is only part of being a mentally healthy person in a healthy family. Work or job satisfaction is also essential. For most people, work gives purpose, meaning and structure to life. We have the drive to learn something, produce something and contribute something. Even if we were rich, most of us would prefer to work. In fact, for even the very wealthy, it is unthinkable not to work even if not for money but in a volunteer capacity.

Although most of us look to our occupation to add a greater dimension, identity and purposefulness to life, some have jobs which are not personally meaningful. How tragic it is when mismatches exist, whether in the home or the job. Love and work—not one or the other, but both. When Freud talked of love he meant affection and when he talked of love and work, he was signifying work that enhances an individual and does not rob him of his loving quality.

The love of man to woman is a thing common and of course, and at first takes more of instinct and passion than choice; but true friendship between man and woman is infinite and immortal.

Plato

COMPATIBILITY—ONE

Ernest Jones, the biographer of Sigmund Freud, the father of modern psychiatry, wrote that Freud was once asked, "When is a person mentally healthy?"

To this he replied, "When he has the capacity to love happily and work contentedly."

To love and to work. How marvelously simple yet intricately complex. Indeed, with this eloquently simple answer Freud had hit upon a central truth. A truth which has become the focal point of a vast amount of naive speculation as well as empirical research.

Our lives revolve around the family and the family around work and love. Thus, in this section we examine some of the factors which have been found essential to mental health, a happy family through intelligent, informed choice of a marriage partner and successful realization of occupational contentedness.

2

Factor A: Let's Go to a Party

Domestic happiness is the end of almost all of our pursuits, and the common reward of all our pains. When men find themselves forever barred from this delightful fruition, they are lost to all industry, and grow careless of their worldly affairs. Thus they become bad subjects, bad relations, bad friends, and bad men.

Henry Fielding

The surgeon deftly makes a cut along the midline of the scalp to the white bone of the cranium. Laying the scalp back, he takes the small electric saw, cuts through the bony structure of the head, and lifts off the dome-shaped bony skull which protected the brain below. Under this protection lies the tough meninges that wrap around the delicate brain like the folds of a diaper on a baby's bottom. The surgeon parts these with his scalpel and exposes the most wonderful of all creations—the human brain. It is more complex and intricate than the most sophisticated computer. Within it are ten billion tiny memory units which can operate at the rate of thousands of times a minute.

The patient is awake and will think and talk during the operation. She will help the doctor locate the diseased tissue. He lightly touches a point in the visual area of the pulsating brain. "What do you see?" he asks. Each person will respond differently, for no two people are alike. Even though, seemingly, all people have similar brains, each is different. At the rear, just under the crown of the head is the visual area; behind and above the ear is the auditory region and on a line from one ear to the other, across the top of the head is found the motor and feeling areas, beginning at the topmost part of the brain. Sometimes an area of the brain is damaged. When this happens, an adjacent portion of the brain tries to take over its function, and succeeds to some degree.

"What do you see?" he asks as he touches lightly in the visual region. The patient laughs, "I see old Spot, the dog I had when a little girl. He's chasing the neighbor's cat up a tree. I hadn't thought of old Spot in years."

The doctor moves his probe a little more to the side and downward. "Now I hear the whistle of the morning train coming into the station. It was the 9:15, but always came through about ten."

The doctor moved the probe to the very top of the right side. "My left foot itches right on the bottom, scratch it please." As the doctor moved the probe a little toward the back of her head, she wiggled her toes on the same foot. "That feels so funny," she said, "just like flies crawling on my toes." The doctor goes on testing out one neural pathway after another in trying to find those pathways that were interfered with by the pathology.

We are all built similarly and, at the same time, differently. There are tiny differences and big differences. If you had been on the operating table and it had been your brain that was being touched, you would have felt, seen, heard other things than "old Spot," for you are unique. There is no one else like you in the whole world, today or in the past. Somewhere there may be a "twin" who looks just like you, and may even have a voice like yours, but under the surgeon's probe would respond quite differently.

In all the ways that you are different, you differ the most in personality. What is personality? Psychologists themselves differ in their definitions. "The general pattern of behavior exhibited by an individual: a unified system of responding," says one psychologist. "The traits, modes of adjustment, defense mechanisms, and ways of behaving that characterize the individual and his relation to others in his environment," says another. "The term personality is used, sometimes interchangeably with ego and self, to describe the highest (and most complex) level of organism-environment integration," contend a couple of others. And, of course, they are right. At the risk of not being so technically correct, personality may be suggested to be, "Your habitual way of behaving."

When Mr. Milquetoast meekly said, "Yes, dear," as his buxom wife hollered at him to take off his shoes before he came into her clean house, we understand something about his personality.

We also know something about the neighbor on the other side when his wife called and asked him not to track mud into the house, if we see him stomp his feet a couple of times and then walk in, mud and all.

Every action, every response, indeed, every thought is part of your personality. Where did you get it? Again, authorities disagree. Those with biological backgrounds point to the contributions of the physical aspects of the body, the neurological, glandular, muscular, and body functioning. Each of these affect the personality. The body varies so much that there are not even the same number of prominent arteries, and their size varies. The great artery which comes directly from the heart and brings all of the blood, the aorta, may have two, three, four, five or six branch arteries arising from it immediately as it leaves the heart. The heart itself is on the left side in some people, in the middle in some and on the right in others. Every other portion of the body has the same types of variances. Each person even has his own "distinctive breathing pattern." Do these biological differences make us personally different? Almost no one would doubt such a contention. It is pointed out that animals, which have few of the learning and environment affects that are experienced by humans, also have different personalities. Thus biologists claim that sociologists and psychologists have emphasized too strongly the learning origins of personality without taking into consideration the physical contributions.

To make it simpler to talk about personality, psychologists classify people into categories which they feel are precise and thus can talk about a limited segment of behavior, or into coarse categories as they deal with more extended bits and sequences of action. These are termed "traits"—such things as generosity, carelessness and sociability. We use these traits to try to describe a consistency in someone's way of acting. But they are not completely accurate descriptions because people are not consistent. One may be a roaring lion at the office, feared by employees, but at home a baby lamb; or one may be completely attentive to his wife when visiting the in-laws—an adoring loving husband—but at a dance may leave her and dance with everyone else's wife.

Just describing a person by using a trait is not completely accurate; we must also mention the circumstance under which he shows it. This, in part, explains why both men and women are different in courtship and in marriage. And the person himself, if he has not been married, will not be able to explain how he will act in this strange, new environment. Thus, promises to "love you forever" are useless. "I'll always adore you." "I'll never treat you like that." These are extravagant promises, like the TV advertisement which promises "the best soap ever made." It's nice to hear the lover make such promises, but they are meaningless. But certainly the man who has been married can promise his bride that he'll never beat her, "I lived with my first wife for fifteen years and never once struck her." But marriage with a second woman is a totally new and different situation. You don't know what you'll do. As one young client said, "Before I married my wife I thought she was sweet enough to eat. Now I wish to God I *had* eaten her."

If we can't depend on these traits under all situations, of what value are they? Even though faulty, they are the best predictors of behavior we have. This is one reason that studies of marriages indicate that those who have the longest engagements, as a group, become the most stable marriages. They have seen their intendeds under more varied circumstances and given them more opportunities to show all sides of a particular trait.

One of the traits which affect the marriage adjustment is that of sociability. There are two aspects of sociability which usually, but not always, go together. One is the *need* for people and the other is the *liking* for them. The *need* for people is an active and aggressive trait which can cause trouble in a marriage, especially where it is high in one mate and low in the other. *Liking* for people is a more passive aspect of sociability and not as likely to cause trouble. Having a strong need for people means that the individual *must* be around others much of the time. Such a person can not be satisfied in an isolated job or where he or she is alone much of the time. For instance there was Michelle:

> I came from a large family. I had four brothers and two sisters. Raised in a small town of the Northwest, we children did most of our playing together. Something was going on all of the time. As kids, we fought and squabbled, played ball and rode the bus to the consolidated school together. I was almost never alone. Even at night two of us slept together.
>
> It was hard to make an adjustment in college because we were not so close together. So, after a couple of years I quit and went to work. In the office there were twenty of us girls. We laughed and talked as we worked. Then I married Phil.
>
> He didn't want me to work so I stayed home. When he left in the morning, everything was quiet—deathly quiet—I just couldn't stand it. I went to the nearby coin-op laundry every morning so I could talk to the other women there. I would go to the shopping Mall just to see people. Have you ever been lonesome in the middle of a crowd? Then I began spending too much money.
>
> Phil and I had arguments. He couldn't understand why I couldn't stay home like his mother and sister. But I just couldn't. I wanted to go back to work, but he wouldn't hear of it because the baby was coming.
>
> I went home to have the baby. Goodness, it was great to hear my younger brothers and sisters fussing again, to hear the door slam and to hear a scream when one kid hit another. I didn't want to go back home after the baby came. I put it off as long as possible. Phil has even offered to buy me a house. What am I going to do?

On the other hand, there are those who have little need for people and like to be alone or with only one or two. The story is told of a pioneer family where the husband came home and told his wife:

"Martha, we gotta move; this country is getting too crowded for us. A new family moved in just twenty-five miles over the mountains there."

During the war, soldiers were arbitrarily assigned to Arctic weather stations where they would see no humans, except the five others who worked with them. Mail and supplies were dropped by plane. Their only contact with the outside world was the mail and radio. Those with high need for people could not stand it, and some even lost their minds. It was found that the only satisfactory way to make such assignments was to select men with very low needs for others.

Women with a high need for people find it difficult to stay home all day. In many cases, it is better for them to work. One source of marriage conflict is where the husband disapproves of his wife's working, when she has this strong internal need for contact with others. It is better for each person contemplating marriage to understand this need in self and the mate-to-be and plan their marriage to set it at ease. If they do not, unhappiness and misunderstandings are likely to follow. As one wife said:

> I am at home all day alone. When night comes and Will gets home, I want conversation, excitement and laughter. I want a few friends in or to go over to visit them. I love to talk, but not Will. He says that he has had a hard day at the plant—and I guess he has. He just wants quiet, peace and rest. He wants to watch the TV or asks me to play checkers with him while he quietly smokes his pipe. Even with his checker moves he is so careful and takes so long I nearly scream. He won't even talk.
>
> It wasn't like this before we married. The last few months of our engagement he came over nearly every night. We went to shows and often to the seashore, snuggled up, and watched the moon on the rushing waves. I should have suspected it when he would say, "I am so content with you by my side."
>
> We almost never went to parties. We didn't even double date. Will would say, "I don't want to share you with anyone." Once in a while we would go to a game, but he prefers watching games on TV. I should have suspected then, but I loved him so. I thought that he was just so devoted to me, but it was just his desire to be alone.

His behavior was just the same before marriage as after. She just interpreted it differently. This is what psychologists call "halo effect." That is, with those we like, we tend to see them better than they really are. We even interpret negative factors as positive, liabilities as assets and bad characteristics as good. For instance, in this case, she interpreted his low sociability as devotion to her. Because of this strong tendency to fool ourselves, we must have an unbiased standard to judge by. This is the value of a compatibility test. Had these two taken such a test early in their courtship, it would have predicted their unsuitability for each other and the unhappiness in store for them.

The opposite type of situation can also bring misery. The sociable man who comes in from work all ready to go places and do things will have trouble staying around the house with a wife who likes quiet and solitude. After asking her to go a few times, he stops asking. Usually it begins with him going out with "the boys" or stopping on the way home "for a beer." Later he spends week-ends away fishing, hunting, at ball games, while the wife is tied at home with the kids. He excuses himself for leaving her with "She won't go, I've asked her." One professional went alone so much that even his friends did not know he was married. It may be only a short step to wanting someone else along. It may not be too much trouble to find someone who wants to go. A businessman or professional may spend more time at his business or office, or he may become involved in luncheon clubs or other organizational activities. Whenever a man spends too much time away from home, you can be sure he is not getting what he wants at home. And what he wants may be people.

Beth has a strong need for people. Wherever there is a crowd, there you will find her. Her mother used to say that she had a wandering foot. After she married Sam, she tried staying at home. It did not take her long to clean up the small apartment and get things ready for the evening meal. Since Sam did not come home for lunch, she had almost the whole day to herself. At first, she would run over to Mary's apartment or down the street to Sue's. But they were busy most of the time with their little ones or fixing lunch for their men.

She joined a bridge club, then a literary group to discuss American Authors—and what Mable, Sarah, John and Bill were doing. She didn't care much about the literature but did enjoy the gossip—if they would just shut up about children and housework; these things bored her. There were a couple of church groups and she invited a few of the other lonesome wives over to her place in the afternoons. By night she had satisfied her need for people and for going. Fortunately, she was married to a man who did not wish to have many people around him.

Since Beth was only average in intelligence, these activities kept her contented. A highly intelligent woman must have more. She needs an intellectual challenge—a chance to use her mind. The other housewives' talk of what little Billy did in the bathtub this morning, how Susie needs to have her teeth straightened, about how tight husbands are with money, the latest movie, or how one can improve cake mixes by adding a couple of tablespoons of cooking oil will not fulfill her mental needs. She can satisfy her sociability needs and the need for mental challenge by taking courses at the local college or university, although one husband did complain about his wife taking home economics and bringing home all the ruined food for him to eat.

These types of adjustments can be made where the compatibility needs are different, but they should be understood and planned for before marriage. A compatible couple may be deeply in love and go through life hand in hand. They never forget how to be attractive to each other. They laugh at the same jokes, share the same ambitions, play together, spend their vacations together and, if religious, pray together.

Others are only married in public. They rush from one cocktail party to another. They dance night after night, spend most of their evenings at the club, take weekend trips or attend ball games. They have made many acquaintances and are continually on the go. They live more in the car than at home and are almost never around when the phone rings.

Either couple can be happy if they are both goers or they both like to stay at home. But when a goer marries a stay-at-homer, trouble and contention are sure to result. The important thing is to know for sure which you are and which your intended is, and plan your lives so that each will be satisfied. It is a tragedy when a pitiable wife is at home alone while the husband is at the lake with his new boat. It is also sorrowful to see a forsaken husband sadly trudging home from work to an empty house, because his wife has gone to visit mother again and will be gone for three weeks. In one case the wife took the children in her camper on a three month's trip through Canada and to Alaska, while her husband remained at home with his work. Maybe they should divorce—well, they did.

On the day that Mr. Franklin retired as Controller of Johnston Manufacturing Company, there were two accountants eager to take his place. Both John Stone and Marc White were well educated with MBA degrees in accounting and each had passed his CPA examinations. The work of each was highly accurate and they were both creative. The president of the company and his Advisory Board debated which to promote.

"Either John or Marc could fill the job, I think," mused the president. "I just don't know which one should be given the job." His wife suggested that they give a party to see which wife would make the better hostess. "The Controller's wife will have to do entertaining," she reminded him.

As most accountants, both John and Marc were less sociable than the average man. John was quite stable emotionally and liked to solve problems, especially tax enigmas. He was tactful in dealing with people, so he got along well with his associates. He and Mary had a happy and contented homelife. She was even less sociable than he but that was fine as he satisfied his need for people on the job and was ready for peace and quiet when he came home. He was glad that Mary was not always pressuring him to take her places or have people in the way Marc's wife did.

Then came the evening of the boss's cocktail party. Marc's wife, being very sociable, was bright, warm and vivacious. She already knew most of the people at the party and felt right at home. Mary, on the other hand, knew none. She was always ill at ease in a crowd, didn't know just how to keep a conversation going, and usually became something of a wall flower. As a result, Marc got the promotion.

Who had made the better choice of a wife? Marc, whose wife constantly nagged him in the home, who forever had the house bulging with company when he wanted relaxation and quiet after a vexing day, but who was an asset at infrequent company parties? Or John, who had a very pleasant home life but whose wife didn't show up well at parties and cost him the promotion?

A nonsocial wife may be a good mate for the man whose vocation is dealing with people if he satisfies his need for people on the job. But he must keep in mind that she will like being with a few intimate friends. Being nonsocial does not mean being antisocial or hating people, nor does it mean being an isolationist or hermit. Nonsocial people are usually so because they are ill at ease among strangers or when around "too many" people. But if a "not too large" group is made up of comfortable friends, neither man nor woman will object. Usually even nonsocial persons are not ill at ease at a family reunion, even though there are many people attending. For the nonsocial person, an evening of conversation, bridge or other game they like with close friends can be a pleasing compromise. More active amusements would, of course, be acceptable to a person who had an excess of energy. Fortunately, sociability problems can most often be solved by the use of intelligence, cooperation and compromise by the husbands and wives.

If this need for people is not satisfied in the marriage, what can be done to prevent a break-up or, even worse, life together in misery? Those who are not yet married and discover a wide divergence in their "people need" may be happier if they find a more compatible mate. For those who are now married and are struggling with this problem, there may be some things which can be done—and then again, it may be too late.

Employed persons who have a high need for people should, in the first place, select vocations which put them in contact with others, for marriages have been broken up by one or the other having a dislike for the job. And people contact can be the thing which is disliked at work.

> Sam despondently plodded into the office of the vocational psychologist.
>
> "I've just lost the sweetest girl in Philadelphia," he moaned. "And I know it's that darn job I've got at the bank. Every night, when I'd come home, I'd be in a bad humor and take it out on Elizabeth.
>
> "When I walked into the house," he continued, "I'd be ready for a fight, no matter what she said or did. If she called out from the kitchen, 'That you, Carl?' I'd holler back, 'Well, who are you expecting, the milk man?'
>
> "Well, when I got home tonight, she wasn't there. A note told me that she'd filed for divorce and gone home to her Dad, and that there was no use of me coming there as she was through. Maybe, if I'd get another job and treat her better, I can get her back. Please help me."

Selecting sales instead of accounting is an example of increasing the contact with people. A few other vocations are listed below:

SOCIABLE OCCUPATIONS	*NON-SOCIABLE OCCUPATIONS*
actor	animal breeder
banker	artist
broker	baker
business agent	bookkeeper
buyer	cabinet maker
chiropractor	cartographer
clergyman	cartoonist
dance instructor	cook
demonstrator	copywriter
dentist	cowboy
entertainer	dental technician
guide	design engineer
industrial engineer	draftsman
manager	editor
orator	electrician
osteopath	farmer
personnel worker	forest ranger
policeman	game warden
politician	lens grinder
president of company	librarian
professor	machine operator
psychologist	machinist

SOCIABLE OCCUPATIONS	*NON-SOCIABLE OCCUPATIONS*
psychometrist	music arranger
purchasing agent	nurseryman
religious worker	purser
reporter	repairman
retailer	researcher
social worker	taxidermist
sociologist	trapper
teacher	typist
union official	welder

Certainly this is not a full list of occupations as there are more than 90,000 by which Americans make a living. These were selected as a cross-section of the occupational life of this country. This list will give the reader an insight into the "people need" of occupations, and the reader can add his into the list in the proper column. Persons with a high need, according to the test, should select a job in or similar to those in the sociable column and ones with a low need, those in the nonsociable column.

Another factor of importance in the selection of a job is the size of the company and the department in which to work. Ask the personnel director about the number of people with whom you will work. For instance, an assembly worker in a large company may be placed in a department of fifty or more employees who can talk and work together. The same assembly job in a small company may be isolated from all contacts with others. A woman working in a large office may enjoy the sociability of a multitude of women and men, but as a secretary for an oil geologist may be the only person in the office other than the geologist, and few callers would enter.

Of what significance is social contact on the job? It may satisfy some or most of the "people need" so that the worker will require less of it off the job. This may make acceptable a less sociable mate. A worker in a less sociable job, on the other hand, will undoubtedly require more social contact after returning home.

The wife who stays at home can constructively satisfy part of her need for people by taking college courses while the children are at school, thus preparing herself for employment after the children are grown and away from home. She can also satisfy this need for sociability by volunteer work at school as a teacher's assistant, in hospitals, with religious or fraternal work, and with organizations such as the Red Cross. Industry is now offering 9:00 a.m. to 3:00 p.m. jobs which are attractive to many.

Several psychologists and sociologists in their research into the causes of divorce have found that boredom is one of the principal causes. Alcoholism and drug addiction is also on a rapid increase among housewives of the middle and upper economic levels, the cause again boredom. Intelligence tests given to housewives in their forties and fifties indicate a deterioration of intelligence because of disuse. A solution to all of these problems is returning to school. Thousands of housewives have solved these difficulties through college classes. Then, too, Boards of Education have set up high school classes for adults both days and evenings. When returning to school, they have been surprised to find others on the campuses in the same age brackets and even older. Colleges, recognizing such problems, will admit women over twenty-one years of age even if they did not finish high school. In this way, women instead of breaking up their homes because of boredom, rather than burning up their brains with alcohol or drugs or allowing them to atrophy through disuse, have found new excitement through learning, new friends through classroom associations and a mental challenge which brings stimulation of the mind and thrills to their whole being.

Both men and women possess the creativity and imagination necessary to solve problems arising from this need for people, if they only recognize the problem. But a multitude of marriages have been destroyed and crashed about the heads of unsuspecting husbands and wives who have failed to identify this basic need in their lives. Not realizing the source of discontent, they have blamed the mate for being uninteresting, when what they were really craving was more human contact—or less of it.

3

Factor B: Freud and Love

Tears, idle tears, I know not what they mean—tears from the depth of some divine despair rise in the heart and gather in the eyes, in looking on the happy autumn fields, and thinking of days that are no more.

Alfred Lord Tennyson

"Forty to fifty percent of those coming into the average doctor's office for treatment do so because of symptoms arising from emotional or mental instability," a famous professor of psychiatry told his medical students. These are people who try to change the deeper desires within from those they think are not socially acceptable into some form of behavior which fits their ideas of what is moral and ethical. Being unable to make the transformation, they substitute other behavior for that which their desires prompt. These we call the unstable people.

People who are not stable are those who are afflicted with what psychologists call "neuroses," if in the milder form, and "psychoses," if of a more serious nature. The one who has a psychosis is unable to make acceptable adjustment to life. This person is "unable to get along adequately in usual environments. Consequently, professional assistance is considered essential, and some form of hospitalization is frequently prescribed."

"Psychotics," as they are called, are frequently met in our society. After all, it is estimated that one out of every ten persons in our population will spend part of his life in a mental institution or undergo psychiatric treatment. Of course, not all who obtain psychiatric assistance are psychotic. Psychiatrists also treat neurotics. When we think of either psychotics or neurotics, we must remember that *their symptoms are just exaggerations of the tendencies of all normals.* Normals have a little of what they have more of. These emotional, and sometimes mental, cases blend in intensity from the normal, who may just have a peculiarity or two, to the definitely "insane." There may be little chance of your falling in love with a full blown psychotic, although it has been done many times. But those who have budding symptoms should be spotted and avoided as marriage partners, if happiness is your goal.

This is not an attempt to make you a psychiatrist, a psychologist, or to teach you how to diagnose mental illnesses. But there are some apparent symptoms that even the layman should be able to spot and know something about. If you should find these in yourself or in the one you intend to marry, you are urged to discuss it with a psychiatrist or a clinical psychologist, but not with a friend who has taken a few courses in psychology and knows all the answers. The professionals are listed in the yellow pages of your phone book.

Perhaps it will be best to discuss the psychoses first.

The most common of all psychoses is schizophrenia. The basic picture in such cases is withdrawal from reality. Most schizophrenics also have a religious-sexual conflict and cannot function properly either religiously or sexually. "An individual who has been *superficially,* at least, intellectually alert, socially active, and *seemingly* emotionally balanced begins to be irresponsible and inaccurate in his thinking processes and to be indifferent toward social obligations and social pressures," is the way one psychologist said it. It begins very slowly and may have been evident in early childhood. As the schizophrenia blooms, he or she does his work with decreasing efficiency, gradually withdraws from social events, and neglects personal appearance and, sometimes, even cleanliness. The person begins to worry about what is going to happen to him. There follows emotional deterioration and apathy, he has less desire to accomplish or to succeed, and then loses interest in the activities going on all around. Many tramps, prostitutes, hippies, and petty criminals are simple schizophrenics, some in the earlier stages.

There are other forms in which hallucinations are present—they see, hear and feel things which are not present. These are often accompanied by paranoid delusions of being persecuted or of grandeur. While some may respond to therapy, it is easy for them to slip back, and some psychiatrists say they are never "cured." One of the authors reports the following case:

> While we were talking to her, she turned her head to the left and vigorously and intensely whispered. When asked to whom she was talking, she answered: "Can't you see him? There he is. It's the devil." Then loudly speaking to the hallucination, "Don't you come any closer. Don't you come any closer. If you do, I'll go get my Bible."
>
> Her husband told how she got out of bed at three o'clock that cold, snowy morning and, with only a flimsy gown on, went down into the cold, dark basement. He awoke and searched for her. There he found her, crouched down in the corner, lips blue, teeth chattering, with a Bible balanced on the top of her head, another tightly clasped to her breast, and

two fingers thrust into her nose. Looking to the left, she pitifully sobbed, "Don't come any closer. Don't come any closer. If you do, I'll tell Jesus."

When asked what the devil wanted, she explained, "He wants to crawl up my nose and get my soul."

Many individuals who are not actually schizophrenic are nevertheless so different, so withdrawn from reality, that although their contacts with reality on the surface remain undisturbed, they are so inadequate that they closely approach schizophrenia. Such individuals are called schizoid. A young physicist who had never had a close friend nor a close attachment with a girl, in fact, without a real interest in people at all, was schizoid. They may accomplish a great deal. There have been many writers, mathematicians, research workers, as well as prominent persons in all occupations, who belong in this category. Although some of them make adequate vocational adjustments, they are quite unhappy. As children they may have been described as lazy, daydreamy, stubborn, or stupid.

The social or economic level of the person is no assurance of his or her stability. While all of those who are shy, withdrawn and have difficulty getting along with the opposite sex are not schizoid or schizophrenic, these are some of the symptoms which attract the attention of psychologists and cause them to look closer. A schizophrenic cannot build a happy, stable marriage.

Very often schizophrenic symptoms are mixed with those of paranoia. People with paranoid symptoms have delusions of being persecuted or of grandeur—either that people have it in for them or that they have unusual talents or are an important person: Napoleon, the president, or Jesus Christ. They cannot usually allow a close, loving relationship with anyone. They are unable to trust their co-workers or supervisors or even their own close family members. They can, and are even likely, to become dangerous and hurt those about them.

Such individuals may engage in unnecessary lawsuits, get into fights over minor causes, and are often the most prejudiced against other groups. Since they are unable to trust anyone, they feel that all Jews, Catholics (Protestants), Negroes, Indians, Italians, Englishmen, Frenchmen, etc. are wrong and will try to contaminate his own particular group. Of course, their own group cannot be trusted either, but they are at least a little more trustworthy. Of course, not all prejudiced people are paranoid, but when they show prejudice against many groups, it shows an indication of that direction.

Another of the types of people who make a poor adjustment in life is the *psychopathic or sociopathic personality.* He or she may be a fun-loving, happy-go-lucky person who is likeable and fun to be with. Reckless—yes—and daring in their pursuits. But they are the ones that the layman may regard as moral degenerates. The first apparent sign is their almost complete disregard for the truth. Most often, such persons have trouble with four tendencies: lying, stealing, alcoholism (and lately, use of drugs), and sexual indiscretions. Swindlers and some criminals are of this type. Men with these tendencies are easier to spot than the women and are less restricted than the women. Most of them have had behavior problems all their life. In school they caused trouble, and few reach twenty-five years of age without having trouble with the police. They may have a sparkling, attractive personality and are often intelligent. They are irresponsible and make their own rules of life, not accepting society's standards. Early in life, when they got into trouble, someone always seemed to bail them out—usually the family. As adults they expect the same thing. Then, after they are bailed out, they are quite likely to do the same thing all over again.

> Sam was such a man. Three times he had been worth more than a million dollars, has had three beautiful young wives, all of whom have had to divorce him, and at the age of forty, is drinking himself to death. He is good-looking and intelligent. He used to work hard as an investment banker. He would work, get rich, fall in love, marry, and have what seemed a perfect economic, social and emotional adjustment.
>
> It was, however, as though he could not stand success. He would begin drinking, become maritally unfaithful, start neglecting his business and go broke again.
>
> His first wife divorced him when he began bringing prostitutes into the home and flaunting his behavior before both wife and children. His second wife divorced him when in a drunken rage he broke a chair over her back. His third wife divorced him when he began to spend on chorus girls the insurance money he was building up for his children's education.

Psychopaths are not thought of as psychotic by professionals. They are found at all levels of employment. Men who become bank presidents and suddenly are found to have a shortage in their books, teachers, laborers and even priests and ministers have been found in this category.

Sexual looseness may not be the result of a high sex drive or need, but an attempt to "buy love." As a young woman graduate student remarked when informed that she had a relatively low sex drive, "Well, I sure have wasted a lot of time in motels, then." When it was suggested that it was not for her own pleasure that she went to motels but an attempt to buy love and affection, she thought a while and then replied, "I guess you are right. It wasn't a lot of fun. Once or twice I got up in the middle and just went home."

It is apparent that such individuals, whether male or female, will not make good marital partners or employees. Tests to measure these psychotic and psychopathic tendencies are not included in the Compatibility Test in this book. They must be spotted by looking for the symptoms. But since such persons are often attractive, charming and intelligent, one must certainly think seriously of these symptoms when appraising a future mate. This is particularly true when they have been divorced one or two times.

There are some other personality defectives that the test will not reveal to you, but they are quite apparent on long association. One must beware of alcoholics—and the incidence of alcoholism among women as well as men is sharply on the rise—users of dope or drugs, habitual gamblers, thieves or those who are continual failures. These last have the "failure habit," and it is hard to break. Such persons may be exciting to be with on dates, or even for weekends, but marriage will bring heartaches and misery.

In the test, we are more concerned with a common group of "unstables" that are found in at least one-half of those with whom we associate in both family and work. The Test will measure this degree of instability, because it contains a gauge of what are called neurotic tendencies (psychoneurosis). In most cases, these can be coped with, if you understand them. Again, as in the psychoses, we all have some degree of neurotic inclinations. The difference between one person and another is the degree to which he is affected. The usual symptoms are *worry or anxiety, feelings of inferiority, frequent fears, self-consciousness, feeling sorry for one's self, and turning emotional stresses into somatic symptoms*—psychosomatic ailments.

Since it is not intended that this become a textbook on abnormal psychology, the person who is interested in a more exact discussion of this subject is referred to textbooks on abnormal psychology, general psychology or psychiatry. These are available in almost any library. Our purpose is to call attention to a quantity of facts which should be considered in the selection of a mate and to impress you with the seriousness of this choice.

Worry and anxiety are common symptoms. Contrary to the opinion of the sufferer, they are not caused by things in the environment; this is true although the one who is worrying can tell you exactly what is causing the worry. But chronic worriers worry even when there is nothing to worry about. As one young worrier said, "I just know things can't keep on going as nicely as they have the last few days. Something is bound to happen. It always does. But what? I'm worried."

This is called *free floating* worry or anxiety. It is floating around inside the individual just waiting for something to happen to which it can become attached—which always comes along sooner or later. Along with this worry and anxiety are usually found irritability, inability to sleep, fast or uneven heartbeats, occasional difficulty in breathing, pressure on the chest, and similar embarrassments.

The early family may not have adequately prepared the child for the life it must face; early emotional conflicts may not have been resolved; there may have been parental inconsistency in word and example; there may have been too little love or too much criticism in the home; the child may have been unfavorably compared with another (Why don't you make good grades like your brother?); impossible or perfectionistic standards of conduct may have been set. Any or all of these may cause one to create a poor opinion of self or feelings of inferiority. These feelings continue into adulthood. Such a fear of failure may be so ingrained into the individual that he may avoid failure by not trying. "One cannot lose a race if he does not run." This not running may become habitual.

Such feelings of inferiority create many problems in life. Perhaps the most serious are two: not liking self and thus not believing that anyone else can like him or her and, second, the tendency to interpret the words of those in the environment—especially the spouse or boss—as derogatory. June illustrated the inability to accept the love of another:

> "It doesn't matter what I do to show my love to June," said the husband. "She still feels that she is not loved. She recently told a neighbor that she had never been loved just for herself. She said that when she was a child, her parents really didn't love her—at least not like they did her sister. 'And now, neither my children nor husband, deep down, really love me. Of course, they try to make me think they do, but I can tell they don't, I know better.' "
>
> June finally filed for divorce. In court the doctor husband told how he had built her three different houses, bought her the finest cars, kept up her club memberships, had taken off from his practice to take her on trips, had tried to do all of the things he thought she wanted, told her of his love and gave her constant attention. "Even now, I am willing to do whatever she wants and am still in love with her." The teenage children verified his statements and added, "We don't know what is the matter with Mama, we all love her." The wife only answered: "He doesn't love me."

We learn to love by being loved. Those who have never experienced love or those, like June, who feel that they have not been loved, do not know how to give love in return. This is the fallacy of those who marry to escape a home situation where there is no love. They want a home and love but without knowing it, they bring a person (themselves) into the marriage who is not capable of giving love or accepting it. This marriage, then, has two strikes against it when the license is issued. A marriage without love is of necessity an unhappy affair.

Then there are those whose only concept of love is what they can get from the other person. As a young man who wore a medallion with the word "Love" upon it said, "I want a woman who wants to do the same things I do. One who can make me happy." In spite of the word on the neck piece, he was a man who was filled with hostility and rebellion toward his home and community and suspicion of those around him. He did not know the meaning of love. To him, it was a way of getting the things he wanted. But this is not true love. Love is working, sacrificing and giving to make the other person happy. A true lover said to his sweetheart, "You seemed so happy yesterday that it made me feel happy just watching you." This is what so many people miss—love is not getting, it is giving. This is the true test of whether you love another or if you are loved. Are your feelings and the actions of the other directed toward bringing happiness to the loved person? Do you want to give or get?

The second facet of a poor self-concept is the tendency to interpret the words and actions of the other as derogatory or blaming. This is illustrated in a couple who had been married eight years:

> It's so hard for me to get up in the morning. I guess I'm just a night owl. I want to sit up at night and finish what I am doing. Then, when the alarm goes off and Leonard has to get up to go to work I just can't get out of bed and fix his breakfast. After all, it's not much trouble for him to fix his own breakfast. He is up anyway. If he loved me he'd let me sleep. I'd do as much for him.
>
> I didn't realize how he felt about it until one morning when he stormed at me: "Why don't you go back to that first husband you loved so much."
>
> I didn't know what he meant and told him so. "You've bragged a hundred times," he scowled, "about how you used to get up at four in the morning and fix his breakfast, and you won't even get up at seven and fix mine. Yet you say you love me—some love."
>
> I got mad at that. I wasn't bragging about it. I was complaining about how doing so had caused me to have to go to the hospital with pneumonia caused by extreme fatigue!

This type of interpreting the words and actions of another is a commonplace neurotic tendency. "If she loved me, she would iron my shirts." "If he had any feelings for me at all, he wouldn't expect me to iron his shirts when my office hours are just as long as his and, after all, I do all the rest of the housework." "If he had any feelings for me at all, he'd phone when he has to be late. Now the supper is all cold." "He doesn't care about me or he'd know I want to get out of this house sometime. He hasn't taken me to a show in two months. All he cares about is that darned TV." "She would rather do things with her friends than stay home with me." These types of instabilities put a severe strain on any marriage and break up some of them. The only defense one has is to understand what is going on in the mind of the other and give reassurance.

Why do people interpret the behavior of their loved one and thus hurt themselves? Deep unconscious pleasures supply every neurosis. Conscious suffering is the exorbitant price paid for these peculiar pleasures. A man asks: "Do you think I enjoy the suffering I get when I think that my wife loved an ex-husband more than she does me?" or a woman incredulously asks: "Do you believe I enjoy my frigidity?" Neither of these *consciously* enjoys being hurt. What they do enjoy is the underlying unconscious fantasies and their self-pity. This self-pity is a precious, enjoyable thing. It is the deepest, sweetest, most alluring of all psychic poisons.

These people are "injustice collectors." They save up and treasure the moments they were slighted and hurt because neurotics unconsciously want to hold on to their inner pleasures. One teacher referred to this collection as the neurotic's "gunny sack." Married couples often hide their grievances. This is called gunny-sacking because when complaints are toted along quietly tucked away for any length of time, they ferment and grow and make a dreadful mess when the sack finally bursts.

Another aspect of instability is frequent fears. Fears of what? Of almost everything. Like the anxieties discussed above, neurotics also have *free floating fears* just waiting until a situation arises to which they can attach. One psychological study of young people of college age indicated that forty percent of them had unreasonable fears. Women had more fears than men. The neurotic, without any fearful situation, can have the same fears that a normal person would if he were attacked by bandits or were about to fall off a building. But the fears of the neurotic come from inside rather than something actually threatening in the environment. They suffer the same physiological reactions as the person who faces an environmental danger: rapid heart beat, increased breathing, tremor and perspiring. It comes as a warning signal that repressed emotional conflicts are about to come to the surface. Extremes of these fears are called *panics.* It is impossible for a normal person to imagine how severely neurotics do suffer.

Love is like food: it matters most when one does not have it. Psychologists are convinced that people are literally starving to death for love. We see youth uprisings because of it, watch TV programs about it, movies based on it, listen to a multitude of songs and near-songs of love and read magazines describing it, all to no avail. This gives credence to the idea that more people are starving for love than for food.

Yet, the capacity to love one's mate is largely dependent on the personal feeling of self-worth. If one does not believe himself worth loving, he cannot accept love from another, no matter how enticingly offered. Confidence that you are an adequate, worthwhile, significant, kind, gentle, loving and therefore lovable human being is so essential to mental health that one cannot adequately function in the unique relationship we call marriage without it.

> A young man of twenty-five had achieved an unusually elevated position for his age. He was a college graduate with remarkable achievement as an athlete; he had struggled and become successful in the business world, and at the time he sought therapy had become a vice-president of his firm. He seemed happily married. To the astonishment of his friends and family, he suddenly became depressed and suicidal.
>
> It was found that he came from an unhappy home; his parents divorced when he was eight; he lived in boarding schools until he was ready for college. He spent a part of his holidays alternately with each parent. His memories of these holidays were filled with recollections of criticism and adverse comment. Each parent would critically watch the growing child for evidence of resemblance to the other parent. When any such behavior appeared, he was unsparingly condemned. He became convinced of his utter worthlessness. He never mentioned his feeling of self-condemnation and futility to anyone—not even to his wife—but it had determined the direction and character of his life.

Many social scientists believe that unhappy marriages begin in the childhood home, and end for the children, almost invariably, in the psychological clinic, with a marriage counsellor or in the divorce court. This places a heavy responsibility upon those contemplating marriage. For your future children's sake you must marry a person with whom you are compatible and can be happy or you condemn those children to unhappiness and suffering. You cannot give to your child a happiness you do not possess. Your own unhappiness will be transferred to children as neurotic personalities and emotional suffering. If you are married now, it means that you are not doing the best for your children to maintain or stay in an unhappy marriage.

As previously stated, when conflicts and frustrations are serious and of long duration and when the anxiety caused by them is not resolved in some way, the body stays in a constant state of tension. After a while, such strain results in certain psychological dysfunctions. These dysfunctions are called psychosomatic disorders or ailments. They are not imaginary, and it is only stupid to think so.

An idea or an emotion can cause stress or a tightening in the tiny muscles of the skin, tissues and blood vessels. This emotion can keep them tight for a long time—an hour, a day, a week, a year, many years. You can't feel or notice them, just as you do not feel the tiny muscles in the skin tightening when you get goose pimples, but they raise the skin and the hairs. If you blush, it is the changing of the tone of the tiny muscles in the blood vessels near the surface of the skin, making them larger, allowing more blood to flow through them. Since this blood is hot, it heats up the surface of the skin, you feel this heat and you know you are blushing. Someone laughs and says, "You're blushing." This causes more emotion, opens the blood vessels a little wider and you blush more. Blood is red, and others see the extra blood at the surface of the skin and know you are blushing.

The same type of thing happens if you feel unworthy or inferior. This feeling is an emotion and it causes certain stresses in your body so one has headaches, ulcers, heart trouble, menstrual cramps, joints hurt or don't want to bend, the stomach does not digest food properly, you are sick. Blood vessels relax, you get hot—fever.

Where the pain or disorder will locate depends on the previous history of the individual. But these psychologically caused disorders—that is, ailments caused by psychological stress—can imitate or develop into almost any ailment of man. Most often it develops into various heart ills, or those of the nose, throat and lungs, or those affecting the stomach and intestinal tract, or menstrual dysfunctions, frequent headaches and migraine, or one or more of the multitude of skin complaints.

Most doctors of internal medicine will admit that at least 60 per cent of the patients they see are suffering from disorders caused psychologically. Many psychiatrists claim that a much higher percent of all sickness—in the ninety to ninety-eight percent range—are caused in this way. It is not uncommon in one psychologist's office, when the secretary comes in with a cold, for him to ask her, "Who are you mad at today?" Hostility, frustration, failure and stress seem to be a basic cause of many diseases.

Almost all people have experienced a time when, under heavy emotional stress, such as fear, anxiety or worry, food seemed to stick in the stomach, refusing to digest for hours. Pleasant emotions, on the other hand, speed up digestion and all body functions. Joy, happiness, laughter, and well-being cause food to be assimilated easier and quicker. Fear, conversely, first affects the mouth, drying the saliva. It acts the same way on the digestive juices of the stomach and intestines, and slows their motility. Thus, a happy life makes for bodily healthfulness. Unhappiness, in contrast, invites disease into the home. Those who feel they are denied love may overeat, become fat, and have even less chance of attracting the thing they desire most—love.

Acne, eczema, neurodermatitis, psoriasis, and urticaria are among the many skin diseases that have emotional causes. A typical case is that of a young woman who had an intense but unsatisfied longing for affection and love. When depressed, she wept, if the weeping was suppressed, she developed urticaria—swelling about the face and eyes.

In picking a mate, if you are a stable person as shown by the Compatibility Test and you select an unstable person who is burdened with worry and anxiety, you can expect doctor bills and sickness in the home. If, in addition, the proposed mate has feelings of inferiority, frequent fears, feelings of being sorry for self, you can usually also expect the sexual problems of frigidity or impotence, for these go together.

If you are the unstable person while the mate is a stable person, you will bring your unhappiness into the marriage and infect your beloved, for unhappiness, like measles, is catching.

If there is instability in one or both of those who intend to marry, what should be done? The ideal solution is to get help from a clinical psychologist or psychiatrist. The next best thing will be to obtain the counselling of a marriage counsellor—not a friend—and perhaps enter into group therapy with others with similar problems.

4

Factor C: Who Is the Boss?

He who forsakes his place as head of the house should not cry when his wife is compelled to take over his duties and responsibilities, and he has to wear the apron. Such a one need not complain when she puts on the pants and orders him about. Neither should he object, when tiring of this farce, she seeks another who is more of a man. For woman is created so that she is not content except she have a strong shoulder to lean upon, a man to make decisions, and a strong husband to look to for protection and solace.

Jobe Feilen

Until a generation ago, the man of the family was expected to be more dominant, the head of the house, the leader. He had absolute control and his orders were seldom challenged. Today, all of this has been changed. There is a greater degree of democracy both in families and on jobs. It has been found that the most effective leaders are those who help formulate objectives, not those who give orders. Why has this change taken place?

Two centuries ago, life was hard. The modern communication and transportation devices that we now take for granted were not even dreamed of then. They also did not have all the tools that have taken much of the muscular work out of making a living. The man worked hard and for long hours to provide food, shelter and protection for his family.

Since life was then predominately rural, the more children a family had, the better off they were. Women gave birth to these children. And, since she was more often pregnant than not, it was unsafe for her to work in the fields. Her primary responsibility was to bear and raise the children until they were old enough to go to work. This was a full-time job, for she did not have any of today's conveniences either. When the boys became large enough, they went into the fields with their father. From him they learned how to perform their roles of provider and protector. The girls stayed in the home and helped their mother while learning their roles in mothering and housekeeping.

Thus boys and girls learned the traditional attributes of masculinity-femininity. They learned early that dominance was a masculine trait, passivity was feminine. Man worked with things, woman with people. One could not understand the thought processes of the other but then there was no need to. Each had his or her own sphere and did not have the time or inclination to try to interfere in the duties of the other.

As time passed and less physical labor was needed in many professions, women began going outside of the home to work. They became their own providers. They needed less protection as the country became more civilized and policemen took over the job. However, since they could not provide for themselves and at the same time have a family, they continued to marry and step into the role of passive womankind. As more and more women began to take over the roles of being their own providers and protectors, they began to question the *right* of men to completely dominate them. The original reasons for such dominance were fast disappearing. During the early part of this century, men began talking with their wives before making a decision.

If marriage were a full-time job of men and women as it was a century ago, its problems would be simpler. But today the husband has full-time work, outside of the home, and his family duties in the home as well. He has responsibilities and loyalties to the employer, his business, or his profession, as well as to his wife. These loyalties create internal conflict. The average man cannot be a truly devoted family man and a dedicated worker at the same time. The more energy and time he devotes to his work, the less to the family. Yet being a good family man also means earning a good income as well as responding to his family.

In most marriages, no wife actually wants complete domination of her husband, not even those who try. She prefers to be married to a husband whom she can respect, who is mature, who assumes the necessary responsibilities of family life and who is considerate of her opinions in arriving at important decisions. In other words, this interrelationship between husband and wife must be one of cooperation rather than competition.

As men are becoming more democratic, the decision-making process is shifting. But really the unhappiest wives are not those who have no voice in decisions but the "forsaken" wives, left with the burden of making all the decisions alone. Well-adjusted wives have "deference and respect for the husband's judgment," and well adjusted husbands show "respect and deference for the judgment of the wife." The final decision is often a compromise, but where each is willing to go more than half way, the solutions are more likely to be pleasing than grudging. In less well-adjusted families decisions become a power struggle. This is especially true in questions which are very important to the two. Complaints as a result of these struggles are principally in these areas: verbal expression of affection, frequency of intercourse, care of the home, sharing ideas, spending family income, spending time at home, personal neatness and appearance.

Soon after marriage, couples are equalitarian—that is, each contributes about equally to making the decisions. Couples even go to the grocery store together and can be seen discussing the merits of a can of peas or whether chicken is a better buy than hamburger.

As the marriage goes on, they may develop their own spheres of decision making. Just as they talk less and less about what has happened to them during the day, they discuss less often their decisions. Since the home and family affairs are the wife's sphere, these decisions are shifted to her and this makes for wife-dominance.

Each person has a certain need to dominate. In some it is strong and in others weak. If one is a dominating individual and the other submissive, this solves the problem of who will "boss." It is the relative strength of dominance that counts. An average man, for instance, might be submissive with a vigorous wife and be very aggressive with a clinging vine. There seem to be at least three things which make one or the other of the pair the more dominating in the home—the actual degree of power, the educational level and the age difference. If one has been to college and the other has not, the one without college training usually feels inferior. The better-educated will even convert the other to his religious and philosophical beliefs. Where one mate is ten or eleven years older, the older one is the more dominant. The one who makes the most money also usually has the balance of power. Not only money but a higher prestige job gives the upper hand to the possessor. Where the husband earns more than the wife, she usually leaves decisions as to investments, real estate and employment up to him. This is part of the balance of power question and should be settled before marriage; this is especially true in a second marriage and can be helped with premarital planning. But normally all earnings of both husband and wife go into the family's general funds to be spent by the two of them.

Ordinarily, a successful man or woman gains self-confidence and skill in managing business affairs. As the community recognizes this success, prestige is also gained in the eyes of the partner. But one study also indicated that the balance of power swings toward the one who participates in more organizations or even goes to church more often. Because of this, power, and with it status, in the mate's eyes can be gained from organizational activities, as much as from paid employment—especially if this is in adult organizations. Stay-at-home mates lose much of this power.

Duties and responsibilities about the house have changed little in the last half century, regardless of feminist movements. Men usually do the heavy outside work as mowing lawns, shoveling snow, putting up storm windows, while the stay-at-home wives do almost everything else. It was found in a national survey that housewives do housework about five and a half hours a day, compared with only twenty-five minutes a day for husbands. The biggest task for housewives is house cleaning (2.2 hours), cooking and dishwashing are next (1.7 hours), and laundry takes 1.4 hours.

One of the extremes in dominance is that where the man takes over all decisions and simply tells the wife what to do. This type of man is rare and is disappearing. The other extreme is the dominant female who may be able to completely dominate her husband, creating the typical "henpecked man." She is gaining in numbers.

Where both are highly dominating, there will be conflict until this power structure is solved. If the man begins to win out, the woman may feel that she is being "possessed." Her husband, of course, will be unable to understand what she means by this (unless he feels he is losing out, then he is possessed), as what he truly wants is a woman who can stand on her own two feet and of whom he can be proud. But she may fight viciously and win, or tear up her marriage, or one or the other may buckle under. This struggle luckily may come up during courtship and be settled, at least for the time being. But it is liable to come up again during the marriage and may continue for years.

If both are powerful and dominating, and one gives in before marriage, there may be rebellion afterwards. This rebellion will cause one or both to be hurt; then disaster may overtake the marriage. It is much better to have an understanding as to the division of responsibilities where each can be dominant in that area in which he or she functions best. Then they can both work together for the same goals and achieve a greater degree of happiness. One kind of compromise may be for each to have a separate career or to be active in different organizations. One twenty-two-year-old college girl said:

> I know the man is supposed to be the dominant one, but I happen to be a dominant female. I've tried to be the submissive one and play the clinging vine type, but it doesn't work. I like directing others' lives, making suggestions and telling them what to do. I want to be head of an organization, chairman of a committee, the "boss." Sometimes I am afraid of being too dominant and try to stay in the background. But other people

seem so inefficient, and soon I find myself telling them what to do. Friends think me a fairly strong individual. They often ask me what to do. I try to tell them tactfully. Sometimes it seems so clear and simple to me, I can't understand why they can't see it.

I also find myself just as dominant with men. I've been told to watch out, "Men don't want a dominant woman." Yet I have no trouble getting dates. A lot of young men—as nice as they are—don't seem to know where they are going. If I get interested in a man, I want to have an active share in his life. Some don't like it, but most of them do.

When I get married, I certainly don't want to wear the pants in my home. I don't want a husband who is "henpecked"—I couldn't respect him. A husband should be head of the house both in theory and in practice. I have found a man who is what I want—I think. He is dominant in a kind of gentle and quiet way. Since I've known Phil, I've learned that a person can be dominant without being domineering.

Those who need to dominate tend to marry those who are submissive. The wife whose submissiveness gets her into trouble needs a forceful man to pull her out.

If two people are compatible, she will be able to satisfy many of his needs and, at the same time, he will be able to gratify many of hers. If these needs are not appeased, there is a temptation to turn to someone outside of the marriage. This is the source of much infidelity. The time to prevent it is before marriage, by seeking someone who will be content with you and one whose needs you will fulfill.

But what of the man who has need to be submissive? This is commonly thought of as "needing a mother." He is likely to marry someone who is a more dominant woman. While this may satisfy his needs and give her what she wants, they will both feel the pressure of society that declares that the male should be more dominant. If either of them is neurotic to the extent of over-valuing the opinion of others—"What will people say?"—it may cause that one to become rebellious and eventually break up the marriage. This creates the problem of the man wanting to be submissive to satisfy his own needs and to be dominant to satisfy the social group. And she will have the opposite conflict. Some people cannot resolve such a conflict. Certainly, as long as the wife's dominance is confined to the house, social pressures are not so great. But some highly dominating women extend their dominion to his work. This can cause others on the job to jeer at him or prevent his promotion. A dominant woman who marries a submissive man must realize that he will probably earn less. His lack of aggressiveness will hold him back. Her interference in his work may cause him to fail completely and finally may bring to pass his giving up even looking for another job.

> I wish my wife would quit calling my office. I've told her but it makes no difference. She calls when her mother gets sick or our son has a fight at school. She also keeps insisting that I ask for a raise; but this is no time for that, they are laying men off. She just can't seem to realize this. She even called the boss one time complaining about my having to work overtime. I think this kept me from getting the last promotion. It has become a joke around the office. The switchboard operator calls out in a loud voice, "Jones, it's your wife again."

Where one is less dominating and powerful than the other, the more dominant one becomes the leader and makes most of the decisions. There is, then, little conflict in this area. If, on the other hand, both are submissive, circumstances force one or the other to decide some things. Even though he or she does not like to do so, some decisions must be made. Here, again, a planning of division of responsibility will be of great benefit. If one knows that he or she *must* make all decisions in one area, it is easier to do. Even though one may not like to do so, some decisions must be made.

The need to be dominating, to be aggressive and to lead is powerful and is highly charged with emotion and feelings. It is not easily controlled or squelched. Indeed, it is so closely related to success in so many vocations that to stifle it may lead to failure.

Being dominant is an asset in many vocations and an absolute necessity in others. Therefore, those in the occupations listed opposite should be encouraged to develop even more of this personal quality. Then, earnings will be more and they will have a better chance of promotion. People with such strong aggressive personalities will be inclined to dominate those with whom they come in contact.

actor
auctioneer
banker
broker
buyer
canvasser
chairman
company president
construction chief
credit manager
crew chief
demonstrator
dentist
executive
foreman
industrial psychologist
interviewer
judge
lawyer
manager
merchant
minister or priest
music conductor
personnel worker
physician
policeman
politician
professor
purchasing agent
radio announcer
reporter
salesman
sales manager
sheriff
ship's officer
showman
social worker
surgeon
teacher
warden
writer
undertaker

These, of course, are not all of the vocations where dominance is an asset, but those who are successful in these are more likely to be strong in this characteristic. Business and professional people who are in direct contact with people in attempting to convince or influence them need a high degree of this trait. Those who direct or control people, either as workers or as clients, must be able to inspire confidence and secure cooperation. This is done by having a degree of salesmanship plus dominance. This will give a cue to the person searching for such a mate the direction in which to look. It will also serve as a reminder to those who feel a need to tell others what to do of some of the vocations they should consider for their own.

A woman can spot dominance in a man who invites her to go to particular places and suggests definite activities when he asks for a date. She can further test him by asking him to order for her when eating or insisting his deciding which show to see, where to go on an engagement, and when they shall see each other again. Men will be advised of dominance in a woman who does not hesitate to take charge of such arrangements and make the decisions. He will also be aware of the presence of this quality in her if she attempts to rule him, always wants to have her own way, tells him what he should do or tries to sell him on making changes in his dress, speech or behavior.

Indeed, this is a most important characteristic in the marriage relationship. It is because of this that a measure of this personality trait is found in the Compatibility Test in this book, and its results must be carefully considered. What happens when two highly dominant people marry?

An irresistible force came crushing against an immovable object, and great was the convulsion. Helpless children, man and woman were thrust first upon one and then upon the other. Tortured feelings, groans and sobs descended on the hapless victims. Shame it was, for this force in another direction could have brought human happiness, and this object been a haven of safety upon which those could have rested their weary bones.

5

Factor D: Don't Be Stupid

The superior man is he who develops, in harmonious proportions, his morals, intellectual and physical nature. This should be the end at which men of all classes should aim, and it is only that which constitutes real greatness.

Douglas Gerrold

One of the oldest and most useful tests of behavior is one which is intended to measure and predict intellectual functioning. The first successful test of this cluster of factors was that produced by the French physician, Alfred Binet, about 1905. This test was designed to sort out the dull pupils of Paris so that they might be trained by different methods of instruction from regular students. Binet observed in his own children that their intellectual capacity increased with age. He reasoned that an intelligent person would be less susceptible to distraction, more likely to adapt to life situations to achieve his goals, and more likely to criticize his own work. These ideas were worked into the first Binet tests.

Practical needs of the U.S. Army during World War I led to the development of the Officer Selection and Classification tests. This test measured the ability to follow directions, to reason, do arithmetic and to recall information. Recent developments have improved these tests and added a few more factors, but they are not noticeably different in content. David Wechsler, of the Bellevue Hospital in New York City, developed a clinical adult intelligence test and extracted eleven intellectual qualities or different intelligences. We do know that there are others which have not been separated, but as we are not exactly sure what they are, they are simply lumped together and called "global intelligence."

There are at least 120 facets of the human mind involving a group of memory factors, four groups of thinking factors, the latter involving mental abilities related to discovering, evaluating, deducing and creativity. No intelligence test that has been built to date measures all of this myriad of qualities. Each test designer selects those intelligences which he thinks most important, according to how the results will be used. This is the reason a person may have one score on a certain mental test and an entirely different rating on another.

The test used in this book evaluates four of these qualities. Borrowing an idea from industrial psychology that an individual should be compared with those with whom he must compete, the mental test used has no age or sex norms. As the husband and wife are in intellectual competition (or cooperation, if you prefer), they are compared to the same standards. It is not meant to be an academic, an industrial or a clinical test. Others are available for these purposes. The test used here gives a rough evaluation of those aspects used most in marriage competition or cooperation.

The rationale behind the use of such a test is that a brilliant woman may not be satisfied with nor respect a less intelligent man, nor will an intelligent man be willing to eternally listen to the chatter of a much less intelligent woman. Since there is some correlation between intelligence and earning power, the woman with both brains and ambition will probably not be content with the "take-home pay" of the mentally deprived man. And, certainly, the man who wishes to climb to the top of the corporation pyramid will need a wife who is mentally alert to handle the required social obligations and to make a good impression on the other corporation executives and their mates and, perhaps, the occasional "out of town" buyer. This mental problem is often faced in marriage counselling. Of course, there are exceptions to this rule:

> The story is told on the campus of a large university of a philosophy professor who is married to a very simple and not very bright wife. Her retardation is so apparent that the professor's friends have asked him why he married her, when he could have selected one more nearly his equal. His answer: "I get all the intellectual challenge I want on the college campus and from superior students. When I come home, I only want a place to rest, a hot supper and love." It was discovered that he had been married before to a very gregarious, vivacious, beautiful woman, who had a Ph.D. and later became Dean of the university. On the other hand, he was nonsocial, shy, a bit dull and had not advanced in the school. Perhaps there were other things also which caused their problems.

There may be an exceptional individual who only wants "a place to rest, a hot supper and love." Such a person can ignore the results of the mental test. But, of course, most of us want a person of whom we can be proud and with whom we can converse about things which are of interest to us. Communication is a major problem in marriage. One of the requirements of adequate communication is understanding of the other. This necessitates similar levels of intelligence.

Wives, too, face the problem of less intelligent husbands. In one of the companies for which we serve as consultant, a brilliant woman had been secretary to the president of this corporation for some fifteen years. Her brightness was recognized to the extent that the president often asked her thinking on problems he had to solve. He also turned projects over to her to organize and handle. She was a power in the organization, and everyone knew it. She attended management meetings and assisted other executives with their tasks.

At home it was different. Her husband of more than twenty years was still a dry-goods clerk. He had not been able to advance even to department head. As a result, he had been reduced in the home to the status of a kept man. He was not involved in the social and business activities of the wife. She had a small business on the side, with which he had no connection. While they lived in the same house, their relations had so deteriorated that they didn't live together. Only her religious beliefs had prevented her from divorcing him years before. Their grown children, who admired and looked up to mother, were tolerant, but had little respect for father.

The strain of such a life of contrasts bore heavily on the secretary. Her doctor believed it was this strain which caused her heart attack at age forty-eight, and the necessity of ending her career at the corporation.

One marriage problem often begins with the wife working to put her husband through college or professional school. He is graduated and enters his profession or job and she is able to quit work and stay home. He must continue to study and learn, thus broadening himself mentally. Not having the challenge of a job, she soon stagnates. Intellectual strength is similar to muscular strength in that if it is not used, it soon atrophies and diminishes. If children come along, perhaps they keep her busy. Her communication is at their level, so she loses the ability to communicate with adults, except about the simpler things of life, over-the-back-fence gossip about how Joey is cutting another tooth and why Susie missed her piano lesson. She has stopped serious reading and studying. But let Jean tell about it:

I worked as a secretary to put John through the long years of schooling, so he could get his Ph.D. in astrophysics. He promised me that I could quit work the day he finished. I looked forward to that day; then I was to go to school. He kept his promise and I quit my job. I was so tired that I wanted to rest a year before going back to school. Then Jamie came, and I was too busy. Two years later, little Elizabeth arrived.

Now, ten years after his graduation, he has made new friends whose conversation is over my head. They talk about things I never heard of. My contact has been with the children and the next door neighbor. I ceased to read and learn. Now, he is ashamed of me and wants a divorce—and I've given the best years of my life to him. Tell me, Doctor, whose fault is it?

Housewives, operators of children's nurseries, grade school teachers and others who spend most of their time with children, often allow their intellectual level to deteriorate until the mate has lost communication. Of course, no one wants to be thought stupid, especially by the mate. And certainly no one relishes the idea of having a spouse of whom one is ashamed. But this is a marital problem often brought to marriage counsellors.

Intelligence is important. It is even more important to those who have ambitious plans and want a mate who will help make these dreams come true—a "helper." To plan, set objectives, conjure up ways to achieve those goals, find methods of getting around the obstacles, meet the disappointments with courage, these require intelligence. It is so easy when conditions become difficult and discouraging to give up and become apathetic. A quick-witted mate to inspire and help solve the problems is a blessing. The small businessman or professional who wants a wife to work with him, or the professional woman who desires a husband to act as business manager, these persons must select carefully, to find not only a mate with sufficient brain power, but one who also has the other qualities needed to serve as a helpmate. And he needs to find one who is at least as smart as himself.

College-trained women of superior ability are sometimes torn between their femininity and intellectuality. And, indeed, it does create a difficult problem. For instance, if the woman is in the top two percent of the population in mental ability, it means that to be satisfied, she should find a mate who rates equally high. This means that on the basis of this factor alone, ninety-eight out of every hundred men are eliminated. This, of course, reduces her chances of marriage.

Women with superior intelligence should not date men who are much less intelligent than themselves. It is too easy to become attracted and "fall in love." If marriage results, intellectual incompatibility will be the outcome. This leads to loss of respect, being ashamed of him and unhappiness. The woman who is afraid of showing her intelligence should remember that less intelligent men will be repelled if she shows her intelligence, but equally capable men usually will not. This is part of mate selection.

Why is it that brilliant women have more difficulty dating and marrying? Some intelligent men who have poor self-images or are self-conscious and self-deprecatory may purposely date inferior women in order to assure their superiority. Later these same men may complain of "feminine stupidity" and divorce their mates. When they date and marry less intelligent women, this leaves their equals stranded. On the other hand, women who have trouble getting along with others, especially men, try to compensate by overachieving scholastically. Thus, their high scholastic accomplishment is a result of meager social life, not the cause. At other times, intellectuality is a defense against the "fear of sex" or "fear of men" or, again, hostility toward men, and this is their way of showing it. If these are not true, there is no reason for a woman to appear dumb. Bill explained his situation thus:

> Elaine and I have been married eight years and have a lot of fun together. She is a highly intelligent woman and I respect her for it. She is a leader in church and community affairs, and so am I. It means a great deal to both of us to have an understanding person to talk things over with. When I have a tough engineering problem, we talk about it and, unbelievably, sometimes she comes up with the answer. It is uncanny. When I get down in the dumps, she cheers me up and reminds me that I'm smart enough to overcome whatever is troubling me. This makes it a good marriage.

Even children notice intellectual incompatibility, although they do not understand what it is. One teenager expressed it this way: "Dad never had any time to do things with Mother. Even on weekends he was always trying to think up new schemes for his business. Often on Saturday afternoon or Sunday he would go down to the plant to try out a new idea. Mother used to gripe about how he never took her out and hardly had time to talk to her. He never discussed the business with her." Questioning the father revealed a lack of respect for his wife. "No use talking to her, all she can talk about is Billy's runny nose. She's not much help, except to cook the meals."

What about the highly intelligent woman, the one who will not be satisfied to talk about "Billy's runny nose?" What is there for her? There are at least two courses open: homemaker and career woman. She can choose either or both.

What about housework? Isn't it dull and monotonous? Certainly it is. But it is no more monotonous than other occupations. For instance, take writing. It may seem glamorous and exciting to sit down to a typewriter and let the words flow out, composing a story or book. That would be great, if it actually happened. But to sit at the typewriter for hours when nothing—absolutely nothing—comes, that's monotony. The writer fears to leave it, for right then an idea could come, and he would forget it before getting back to the machine. Sitting there typing when the sun is shining, the trout are biting, a great day for golf, the big game is on, that's dull. The rewriting, four, five, six times to change a word, to create a better sentence, changing a paragraph into a sentence, this, too, is monotonous.

The bookkeeper and accountant who search hour after hour for a three-cent error, the concert pianist who practices seven hours every day, year after year, that is real monotony. The professional football player running the same play Monday, Tuesday, Wednesday, Thursday, Friday and Saturday, hoping to use it on Sunday, has only one hour a week of excitement. Every career has its monotonous times. When giving flying lessons, the instructor explained flying as "long stretches of monotony broken occasionally by seconds of sheer terror." Many housewives seeking to get away from the monotony of their work have taken jobs only to find them even more confining, dull and monotonous than washing dishes or dusting. And, on the job, you cannot break it by phoning a friend or running next door for a cup of coffee and a little conversation or even turning on the radio.

> John Robertson looked back on his life as a grocer the day he retired. "What have I accomplished in these fifty years of hard work?" he asked himself. "Seems as though I've only made a living, although at times a good one, and saved a few dollars for old age. But what have I contributed to the world or society? Nothing."
>
> His wife, on the other hand, looked at the three sons and two daughters she had borne, raised and developed. Through them and their careers, she had helped to feed an undeveloped nation in Asia, taught in a university, built automobiles, defended the poor and defenseless in courts, bound up the wounds of soldiers on the battlefield and brought nine grandchildren into the world. Her life had been one of achievement and contributions to the betterment of the world.

In raising her children, she had done the work of a teacher, a minister, a judge, a psychologist, and a dietitian, and had worked harder than her husband. Since she would continue working after his retirement, working longer hours and more years than he, she would live longer.

Woman looks at a home differently than a man. It is an extension of herself and her personality. She looks upon a dirty floor or dishes as a flaw in her being as a human. But to the typical man, home is a place of relaxation from the tensions of life and the competitive battlefield, a place of renewing of courage and spirit.

On the other hand, an intelligent woman can seek a career. In past ages, she had to do work similar to housework in finding a job: maid service, dressmaking, nursing, teaching, cooking or such occupations. This is not true today. The intelligent woman can aspire to the highest positions in industry, the professions and politics. There are women chief accountants, legislators, managing editors, senators, heads of government bureaus, corporation directors, managers, and several presidents of multimillion dollar firms. These women did not get there on looks or sex appeal but by virtue of talents, ambition and sheer determination. They are not only heads of companies serving women's needs, as cosmetic and clothing manufacturing, but they also head firms producing airplanes, oil well machinery, drug chains, beverages, bronze castings, and others.

The woman of the future will likely have two separate careers, one as a homemaker and the other in business, industry or the professions. While her children are in grade school and junior high, she can return to college and prepare for her own career. Colleges already are feeling the effect of these mothers in their day classes. She will have sufficient time to get her degree and even do graduate work. Then, when the children no longer need her, she will be young enough to get into a satisfactory career. This schooling will do more than prepare her for a career. It will keep her from becoming bored and lonesome during these child rearing years. It will also keep her mind strong and active, preventing its atrophy, as so often happens when she thinks and talks only on a child's level. It will make her more interesting to her husband and friends and prepare her for when she no longer has the children at home. It will enable her to contribute materially toward the spiralling costs of education for her children. It will give her a sense of worth instead of debasing her to the status of a babysitter for her grandchildren. This alone could decrease a growing social problem in this country: alcoholism and drug abuse among housewives. Furthering her education, she will not likely be driven into either by boredom.

Intelligent women have trouble settling into the secondary place into which they are forced by marriage. This certainly is one motivation behind the feminist movements. It is also an important reason for the skyrocketing divorce rate. For centuries, women's brains have been ignored. These minds are now demanding expression. Women have been considered a minority group although there have been more of them than men almost every year since the Civil War.

Society's attitudes are changing. Housewives who hold jobs or enter professions are not so strongly criticized, nor are their husbands condemned for not supporting their families. Women are needed in industry and are receiving promotions to managerial and executive positions. One of the authors recently spoke before the Management

Club of an aviation repair depot. Almost half of the 1,500 members were women. Top management credited them with doing an excellent job. Although, nationwide, women are not receiving such recognition, that day is fast coming.

But to get back to our theme of intellectual compatibility. If the man and woman should by some chance not be equal, under what conditions can they make the best adjustment? It is usually better for the man to rate higher for a couple of reasons: in the first place, in our society, he is still regarded as the principal breadwinner. The more intelligent he is, the more successful he can be. And certainly the wife will not begrudge him this one measure of superiority, if he will bring in a larger part of the earth's wealth. The second reason is that a woman is usually much happier if she is able to look up to her husband and respect him than if she has to look down on him as a dumbbell.

What if she selects a career and earns more than he? Our changing customs and mores are accepting this, as long as both the man and woman can learn to look upon all family earnings as "our earnings" and not as yours or mine.

6

Factor E: Let's Go to Bed

The sexes were made for each other, and only in the wise and loving union of the two is the fulness of health and duty and happiness to be expected.

William Hall

Sexual need or passion is a mysterious something which has brought ecstatic joy to the human race, but not only joy but also the sufferings of hell. This need for sexual expression is not a fixed thing, the same from individual to individual. It differs as much as the size of the sex glands themselves. It varies from the individual who hardly feels it flutter to the possessed individual whose life is under its domination. Studies have shown that this need for expression fluctuates from less than once a year, in the persons with least need, to scores of times a week in the most possessed.

Janice was a passionate woman. She averaged forty-five to fifty orgasms per week and, in one week in which a count was kept, reached a hundred and five. Her need was so great that she was largely controlled by her sex desire. Yet she did not have a pathological condition nor was she a case of nymphomania. These were her natural sexual needs and desires. It would have been absolutely impossible for her to have made a good marital adjustment with the average man. In fact, she had tried with many men, but had not succeeded. But there are men who would have suited her exactly.

Marriage counsellors generally conclude that no couple can make a happy adjustment where the drive of one is high and the other is low. This seems to be true regardless of their educational level, social or religious backgrounds, or how hard they try. They may not get a divorce right away. Certainly, many of these mismated couples stay married and true to their marriage vows for years, or until death. Though some of these are able to make tolerable adjustments to this incompatibility, they usually do not have the happy marriages they had hoped for.

One of the tragedies which appear in a number of marriages originates in the fact that the male is usually most desirous of sexual contact in his early years, while the response of the female is still undeveloped and inhibited. Most studies suggest that the female does not reach sexual maturity and peak of need until the late twenties or early thirties.

The predominant sexual problem of the American female is frigidity. Estimates of the incidence of frigidity is two to ninety-eight percent, depending on whether the person giving the figures is a gynecologist, with his physiological biases, or a psychiatrist, with his psychological biases.

Only a small percentage of frigidities are caused by physical factors such as an imperforate hymen or insufficient hormones. Some cases of frigidity which cause physical pain are due to what has been called "organ language." That is, the sexual organs are saying what the woman does not dare say: "I don't want sex," or, "I don't want sex with you." The pain gives an acceptable excuse for refraining. What can the poor woman do? Neither she nor her doctor can cure this type of apparent physical frigidity.

Most couples reduce their sexual activity after the female has felt pain on several occasions. This avoidance of sex increases until sex is stopped altogether. This often seals the doom of the marriage.

As is true of most sexual problems, in both men and women, the real cause is psychological. This may be a result of improper training. If there is a severe conflict between what the woman has been taught or has had ingrained into her mind, and what is expected in a marital situation, the result often is frigidity. Frigidity may express itself in several ways: a desire to escape sex altogether, the lack of feeling during intercourse, or attempting to enjoy sex but not reaching orgasm.

Contrary to what one would expect, women who have escaped by one of these routes are often the sexiest looking and acting, dress enticingly or are exhibitionistic. Go-go girls and strip teasers often belong to this group.

Our changing mores and attitudes toward sex and the gaining of freedom by females are creating situations not faced by former generations. For instance, young people of today are engaging in premarital sex and living together without the intention of marrying each other. If they have a good sexual relationship together without marriage, once they get married, the new relationship often seems to fall apart. Most young girls enjoy being courted and sought after even if they don't really get much from the sex act. They are often just buying affection or rebelling against family and society. Where they are having a good sexual life, it may be because it satisfies certain conscious and unconscious feelings of hostility toward parents and society. In these cases, tabulations point to the increasing percentage of frigidity in the female and impotence in the male when they marry each other or other mates "for keeps." For some reason or other, the institution of marriage changes things.

The unmarried young woman is more and more often approaching the family physician and psychiatrist with problems arising out of this newfound sexual freedom. Some of the problems the single woman presents, are:

1. Emotional trauma due to forbidden sex. She shows symptoms of mild anxiety to deep depression. She comes for help but is also seeking approval. Since doctors are not moral judges, they try to help her explore both the advantages and disadvantages of her behavior and make her own decision.

2. Contraceptive prescriptions. Most doctors are now giving advice and the "pill" to those who come. They have learned to cover themselves by asking the leading question, "You are planning to be married, aren't you?" If he is the family physician, he usually discusses the psychological consequences of her behavior.

3. Unmarried pregnancy. Modern doctors usually do not recommend marriage to the young teenager, but point out that most teenage marriages fail, especially where a pregnancy has occurred. On the other hand, if the girl is stable and engaged and the boy can support them, they usually are willing to approve the marriage. Otherwise they will point out to her the advantages of giving the baby for adoption.

In contrast to these complaints, the complaints brought by married women are somewhat different.

1. The husband is oversexed. Many women feel that their husbands want what they regard as excessive sexual activity. This feeling on the part of some wives is because they get little or nothing from sex. With others, it is because of prudish ideas of what is normal. The doctor in these cases must do some re-education. Most women believe their man is getting more sex than he actually is, and most men believe they are getting less sex than they actually are.

2. The husband is undersexed. Sometimes the wife feels that the husband has lost interest in sex and therefore fears that he is sick or that there is another woman. Very often, the truth is that he has just given up after a long battle with a woman who has retreated into partial frigidity.

3. The husband is homosexual. Often this is where the husband attempts some experimentation of which the wife disapproves, or there are some cases where the man is bisexual. If the doctor can help her understand her husband

and his problems, it can help. She may be able to increase her own activity in both quantity and quality and make the home a more pleasant place, and make him a better husband. She may then consider these episodes of his as of less importance.

4. She is frigid. Some women have regarded sex as their duty and for the husband's pleasure. They then grow to resent it and often seek help in finding enjoyment for themselves, which may require sexual re-education or psychotherapy.

Many men also seek to avoid sex. The male equivalent of frigidity is called impotence. Research studies indicate that sixty to seventy percent of adult males have it to some degree.

By impotence is meant the inability to have complete intercourse. This is painfully embarrassing for the man. For, while a woman can fake it, a man cannot. Nothing hurts a man as much as for the woman to disgustedly remark, "And I thought you were a man," or some such expression. She did not need to say it, as he has already called himself several names. As Vic said:

> I have been married just two weeks, and Babbs is the most beautiful girl I've ever seen. It all started on our honeymoon, the second day. Babbs and I went to bed. We kissed and petted and said endearing words, but nothing happened. We worked at it for an hour, but it was dead.
>
> As soon as we came home, I went to our family physician. He gave me a couple of hormone shots, they worked for a couple of days, then—nothing again. But, gosh, doctor, I'm only twenty-seven years old and I love my wife. What can I do?

Psychotherapy helped his neurosis.

In spite of all man's bragging and mostly lying, "I always go back a second time;" "I never miss a night;" "I can go all night;" men are very often less sexually capable than women. Sometimes when husbands are too tired, worried, under strain, mad at the wife (or someone else), sick, or occasionally for no reason at all, they just can't do any good.

This can do at least three things to the man. It can break down his confidence in himself; it may make him afraid it will happen again next time (and then it is more likely to) and it may cast doubt on his own manhood. The strain of these effects may make him miss again and again.

If he loses his confidence, he certainly cannot respond. In the sexual area, as in other areas of life, "What you think you can do, you can." This fear of "not being a man" is in the breast of nearly every male, regardless of his station in life or age. As a seventy-year-old man said to his doctor, "Doc, I'm afraid I'm losing my 'Nature,' can't you do something for me?"

Physicians in general practice list as the sexual problems for which men most often consult them the following:

1. Partial impotence. Less than 5 per cent is due to organic causes. Questioning usually reveals that there are also other marital problems. Which comes first, the sexual or the other problems? The doctors themselves do not agree on this. But when these men see the physician, these problems are usually all tied together. This impotence is also due to the approach of middle age with its financial worries, teenage problems at home, frustrations, anxieties, sense of being a failure, realizing that earlier life goals may never be reached, fear of unwanted pregnancies, a privacy problem, coupled with an unrewarding sexual adjustment. Studies have shown that these are the same ages at which marital infidelity is most likely to occur, starting at age 35 to 45 in women and 40 to 55 in men. This is a time of one's reassessment of life. Earlier, the individual expected to conquer the world; then the realization crept in that this might not happen. Then, too, these people look forward to the fast-approaching old age and feel they should do something about it. A poet called these the "foolish years."

2. Venereal disease, especially gonorrhea. One doctor said he had been able to help the men get by with it at home by blaming it on getting drunk and being away from home. He intimated that he didn't know how he would handle it if an infected husband came to him who was a "teetotaler" and never went out of town. He also admitted that he had had one or two cases where the wife had become infected while the husband was out of town.

3. Men concerned with the size of the penis, about its being too small. Studies show that while the penis varies much in the non-erected size, it is remarkably uniform in the erected size. In almost all of the cases where the men complain, the wife does not regard it as too small. In fact, an understanding of the female physiology indicates that the satisfaction of either the man or the woman is affected little, if any, by the size of the penis.

4. Men who have some physical disablement or deformity. Doctors usually recommend that they experiment with different techniques and positions until they find what is best for them. In this matter of positions alone, one writer claims to have learned of 2,496 different ones. Somewhere in this great number should be one to please any arthritic, paralytic or otherwise handicapped person.

5. Perhaps of all those who are afraid of sex, heart patients lead the list. Usually it will not hurt. It should be noted that 80 per cent of those men who have died during intercourse were with someone else's wife!

6. Premature ejaculation is another type of impotence. The man becomes excited and anxious; he has no trouble with erection. But as he approaches or begins his thrusts, ejaculation occurs and it is all over. The woman is left aroused, ready, but unsatisfied. Some men have claimed that it is because they are so highly sexed, but this is not true; it is a form of impotence.

In the same way, the "chaser" is not usually a highly sexed individual but more often an impotent one who is looking for a woman who can make him perform.

> Jack was known by his acquaintances as a chaser. He made passes at every woman he met—young, old, fat, skinny, beautiful, or ugly. His wife pretended that she did not know about his escapades, that is until she drank too much at a party one night. Then she shocked all of her friends by crying out at him: "You dirty bum, you chase every woman you see but can't even take care of your own wife."

These are all different forms of the same disorder: impotence. About five percent could possibly have physical causes such as past or present infections. The others are emotionally caused. This is one way that a man can express his hostility toward a woman or toward all women. He punishes her by denying her satisfaction. With premature ejaculation, he can receive his own pleasure while punishing the woman. In other forms of impotency, the man is willing to even sexually starve himself in order to vent his hostility and get revenge. Most men do not know the dynamics behind their impotency and protest their desire for normal relations.

> Fred, as a boy, was raised by an aunt whom he hated. His feelings were so intense that he had attempted to kill her when he was a young man; but the attempt failed. Several years later, he married. It lasted ten years, then he divorced. Two years later he remarried.
>
> "For years, I've had trouble with sexual adequacy. Not all the time, but occasionally for weeks at a time. I notice I have more trouble when the wife and I have an argument, a disagreement, or she does something that I don't like."

Unfortunately Fred was not only punishing his wife for displeasing him, but also venting some of his hostility toward *all women.* This hostility was acquired from his childhood relations with the aunt.

Nature must have intended sex for man's pleasure even though there have been those who preached that it was only for procreation. If it had been designed only to produce offspring, a simpler method could have been used. For instance, a multitude of nature's creatures produce their young by simply dividing into two beings—daughter cells, they are called. This would have made it so simple.

Or Nature could have made man so that the female would deposit her eggs outside of the body and the male would then fertilize them in their nest. This would eliminate all intimacy, all problems of getting along, marriage, divorce and rape. Human beings could have been made like that. Or, like the queen bee, a woman might produce any number of children after only one intercourse. With the bee technique, all of these children could be produced without her ever again being "bothered by a man."

But Nature has done more than just give men and women the potential for joy through sex. It has demanded sexual outlets. If the individual does not voluntarily comply, Nature has its own way of insisting upon and punishing noncompliance. The female who denies herself may be punished with "pruritis vulvae," which is an intense itching of the genitals. This demands scratching and douches. As an example of this, one doctor prescribed douching three times a day and rubbing a lubricating cream on the parts "after each meal and before going to bed," for a maiden lady of forty-five who could not, as she called it, touch herself. She was also told to insert suppositories four times a day. This activity cleared up the itch by relieving some of her sexual energy.

Many of the emotional and sexual problems of both men and women are the result of denying Nature's demands. For instance, a nagging wife may be one who is suffering from insufficiency or sex starvation. She may be denying herself through frigidity. Sometimes, the husband, who may be the cause of the nagging, gets tired of it and divorces her—thus punishing her even more.

Other women, as a result of this denial, are constantly sick, have headaches, or go under the surgeon's knife. Joanne was a good example. She had already had eleven operations. Her abdomen, with its scars, looked like a road map. She was referred for psychological treatment because she wanted another operation. This time it was to have a kidney removed. Seven doctors had told her it was unnecessary and dangerous. So she continued traipsing to another and another. Before psychological treatment had had a chance to help her, the thirteenth doctor agreed to remove it. To her, this was better than having sex—dirty sex—with her husband.

Nature seems to delight in inflicting headaches, cramps, dizziness, pain and itching upon those who disobey her, men and women alike.

Sexual problems and emotional problems are closely related. Which causes which? This is similar to the old question of "Which came first, the chicken or the egg?" It has been found that there is sexuality in childhood. When its effects are misunderstood by either the child or his parents, neurosis can result. It must be pointed out that all of us, even the most emotionally balanced, have neuroses in one area or another. Sex is the area most affected by these neuroses as sex permeates our entire lives. Whether sex caused the neurosis or a neurosis caused the sexual problem is of little importance. The important thing is to remove the neurosis and thereby make a better adjustment in *all* areas.

To have a good marriage, two people must make a satisfactory sexual adjustment, not what is considered a satisfactory adjustment by some experts, but what is satisfactory for the two of them. What satisfies and pleases the two partners is all that matters. This does not occur just as a happening, or like lightning striking when they kiss or touch each other. This sort of thing happens in the movies or in a novel, not in real life.

In order to have a satisfactory adjustment at least two things are necessary: First, the two should have a *similar* sex drive. Whether it is high, low or somewhere in the middle is not important, as long as they both are in the same range. But for one to delude himself or herself into believing that it is possible to diminish too strong a sex drive or to pep up one that is too low is a self-delusion and only leads to unhappiness. The test of heterosexual need will indicate the strength of your drive and that of your intended. Do not ignore great differences.

"The only way I'll continue to live with her," Mark told one of the authors, "is if she will agree to my having girl friends on the side. No one woman is enough for me."

Asked why they had married in the first place, June told how they used to visit a neighboring city on weekends and check into a motel.

"We had so much fun together on these weekends that we just decided to get married."

Mark had a very high sex drive and June a low one. Being together every weekend was all right but when they were married and every day became a weekend, their troubles became apparent. Now they faced a crisis.

It sounds cold-blooded to many youths to tell them that there are millions of people in this world with whom they can make a marital adjustment or that one should pass up the impossibles. This caution is more apt to be listened to by those who have been married and divorced or widowed. And, after all, it is more important to them as they are facing their second and maybe last choice. Young people will often insist on finding out for themselves.

But there is a second consideration. Even though you and your mate may measure exactly the same in this quality, you may still have mating troubles. Either or both may have emotional problems buried deeply within, and which may not be apparent or of which you may not be aware. This will not be known until after marriage. Even sleeping together or living together for a short period will not usually reveal them.

In our culture, the emotional aspects of the sexual drive, in both male and female, are just as important and sometimes more so than the physical. Emotions can have a sufficiently powerful effect as to cause sexual activity even when the physical is not aroused. When the physical is aroused, it is much easier for the emotions to drive the individual toward sexual activity. In measuring sex drive, the combined effect of the physical and emotional are evaluated. Emotions are affected by reading sexually charged material, viewing pictures or persons that are sexually stimulating, coming in contact with or being around an exciting individual, being in a place or under conditions where sexual activity has taken place in the past or just thinking about sex.

When two people are in love or are attracted to each other, a kindly word, touch, holding hands, a stroke of the hair, embrace, or even sitting close are also sexual in nature. They are physical manifestations of love and should be engaged in often by husband and wife. A man can show a woman that she is desirable, for instance, by gently and lightly touching her around the neck region or on the ears. This has an emotional effect, turning the mind toward love and its expression. Failure in this area often turns a woman cold. One husband, a patient, came home from work in a critical mood. He blamed his wife for having a cluttered house, censured her for the way she corrected the four preschool children, and reproved her for her cooking, then could not understand why she rejected sex after they went to bed. He did not understand the need of a woman to be shown love.

"Women give sex to get love. Men give love to get sex." Understanding this difference in attitude can help each to comprehend the other. This, too, will give both the man and woman the key to get what he and she needs to feel fulfilled. For instance, it will teach a man that to arouse a woman, he must say with both words and actions: "You are desirable." For, while men are erotic, women are romantic.

The rule for satisfactory sexual adjustment is patience, love and mutual assistance. This is one of the biggest voids of today. Patience and consideration are not virtues that the male is taught. In daily life the male is supposed to be quite aggressive and competitive, to show accomplishment and speed ahead. He brings these same qualities into the bedroom. Many sexually frustrated women with deep sexual feelings are completely stymied by unknowledgeable husbands—those who know nothing about making a woman emotionally receptive. Men study for years to prepare for a career, but feel that it is not necessary to read a single book in preparation for a more important part of their life—the marriage. But with or without books, patience and consideration, really *caring* about the partner is the important thing in sexual adjustment.

What should a couple, with similar sex drives, do if sexual problems show up after they are married? Not run for the divorce court as some have, or feel that the marriage is damned. Read this chapter over several times and then begin working on the solution. This will require love and patience on the part of each. Many couples have found that it takes months or even years to make a complete adjustment. All that you should ask is that you are making progress and are improving.

The sexual drive manifests itself in other ways than solely a need or desire for release through sexual practices. It affects every action of the individual, especially the social relations with other persons of both sexes. Frequently, persons with higher drives enter such social service occupations as doctors, nurses, biologists, psychologists, ministers, lawyers, social workers, teachers, psychiatrists, masseurs, etc. Of course, just because a person is in such an occupation is no guarantee of a high drive. Some go into psychology, for instance, hoping to cure a maladjustment or the ministry hoping to be "saved." There are other reasons also; family background, social or family pressure, prestige, financial reasons or pure accident.

Thus, one may utilize part of the sex drive (or sublimate it) in the vocational life. Such a person may need to marry a spouse with a lower sex drive. A gynecologist, for example, would have less sex curiosity at home than a bricklayer. Work provides a partial way of escape for those couples where one has a higher sex drive than the other. This seems to be about the only sublimation that actually works.

What if, after studying this chapter and working on your sexual problems, you find you are not making progress? It is then time to seek professional help. A clinical psychologist or a psychiatrist may point the way. This seeking help is easier for the woman than the man. One husband who was very dissatisfied with the way things were going made the foolish remark, "I don't need any doctor to tell me that I love you. If you would just act like a wife, everything would be all right." In such a case, the woman must cajole, encourage and entice him toward the doctor's office. Of course, if you had a heart attack, he would quickly call a doctor. How much more important it is to seek help in the area which controls so much of the future success and happiness of both.

"The bedroom is a play room. The couple should relax and enjoy it. Variety is the spice of life and this suggests experimentation and anything goes as long as it is acceptable to both."

There are three factors conducive to the enjoyment of sex:

1. The couple must be emotionally mature, must know themselves and their partners, and must have mutual respect and trust for each other.

2. Both of the partners must feel comfortable about the level of sex in which they are engaged. If one thinks of it only as a physical thing and the other believes that sex is right only as part of a deep spiritual love, they would do better not to go to bed. Women usually want a man who does not separate sex from love.

3. There should be good communication of both verbal and nonverbal nature. They should tell each other what excites, what inhibits and where and how to do what. But, of course, there cannot be communication in the bedroom if there is no communication in the living room.

Many authorities consider heterosexual compatibility the most important. Without compatibility here, your chances of marital happiness are greatly reduced.

7

Factor F: Human Dynamos

The longer I live the more deeply I am convinced that that which makes the difference between one man and another—between the weak and the powerful, the great and the insignificant, is energy—invisible determination—a purpose once formed, and then death or victory.—This quality will do anything that is to be done in the world; and no talents, no circumstances, no opportunities will make one a man without it.

Sir Thomas Buxton

What man has not said, "If I had money I wouldn't work so hard?" And yet most of the wealthy men and women work harder than the average laborer. Thomas Edison, for instance, after he had invented over a thousand things, such as the electric light, dictating equipment, moving pictures and the phonograph, inventions which advanced our civilization immeasurably, after he held these patents and could have lived extravagantly the rest of his life, it is said that he worked twenty hours a day and created another 1,500 inventions. The question is often asked why so many wealthy men continue to work sixty to eighty hours a week. The answer is simple: they can't help it.

There is an inner force, drive or push which makes some men and women continue to work hard regardless of money or position or need. There are women, for instance, who drive themselves day and night in philanthropic endeavors where they derive no income.

This push is so intense in some that they can hardly sit still even to read a book or hold a conversation. They are floor pacers. Some wake up in the middle of the night, get up and work for an hour or so, then, perhaps, go back to bed.

The wife of a minister recalled that her husband often awoke in the middle of the night and wrote his sermons. The best sermon he ever preached he wrote lying on the living room floor at three o'clock in the morning. A police officer tells of an office on his beat where he sees the light on at all hours of the night. The first time was a cold winter night when he passed at four-thirty in the morning and found the light on. As he approached, he saw a shadow cast on the frosted glass of the door. Knowing that money was sometimes kept in that office, he felt sure he had a thief. But it was only the businessman, working on a deal.

> Bill was the most energetic man I ever knew. He pastored a large city church—one that he had built. He not only did an excellent job as minister of that church, but also spoke for one of the car manufacturers, as part of their public service program. Often he would leave his home city on Sunday evening, fly to a distant speaking engagement, perchance, as a keynote speaker for a convention early Monday. He might speak two or three times in various cities before returning to his church for the Wednesday evening service. Such a schedule he maintained for years, not even taking a vacation. In addition to this, he was working on a book in his "spare time."

Somewhere within man this energy is produced or obtained. Biologists indicate that it is a chemical process, instigated by the glandular secretions and having to do with the hydrogen ion, but they don't know exactly how. Dieticians sometimes admit that some people produce more energy than can come from the food and drink intake. They use more calories than is in their food.

The puzzle is not solved, but there are those who have an excess of physical and nervous energy. Those who rarely ever get tired, who seem to be able to go on day and night, outwork other men or women and keep going . . . going . . . going.

This excess of energy is both a blessing and a curse. It is a blessing in that it will allow possessors to work harder, and faster, and longer than others. If they do tire, many of them have learned to close their eyes and rest, or sleep, for a few minutes—fifteen, twenty or thirty—then they are ready for another day's work. Such people, as they get older, retain a more youthful body, so that one who is sixty can often outwork the average man of thirty-five.

> Dr. Jones taught anatomy, histology and eugenics. In addition, he carried on extensive research. He was also on the staff of a 200-bed hospital as pathologist. But research was his first love. From the time his classes ended about four in the afternoon, he worked in his laboratory. He took out time for a sandwich and cup of coffee at seven, then back to work. At one in the morning he would retire. When on an exciting problem, he would not go home, but lie down on the laboratory table for four hours sleep. Then up at five and back to work. Just before his eight o'clock class he would allow himself a twenty-minute nap on the table, and another at twelve. Sometimes he would keep this up for a week or ten days without going home. He went only to class, the laboratory and the hospital. He

explained, "I've got work to do." He wasn't exactly a young man, having already passed his sixty-sixth birthday.

Another characteristic of this excessive energy is that it accentuates any other qualities in the individual. For instance, if one has a higher than average sex drive, it will make such a person more energetic in his sexual activities. One such person could continue for an hour to three hours. Another such man who was 73 years of age still desired intercourse three times a week. On the other hand, a depressive individual who has this elevated energy level is liable to suicide.

Frank rushed into the office early Monday morning and slammed an automatic pistol on the desk of one of the authors.

"For God's sake doctor, keep that gun for me for a few days. I have such a strong urge to use it. And, can you have me locked up in jail for a couple of days? On my way to your office, I passed the Hilton Hotel and had a compulsion to rent a room on the top floor and jump out of the window."

The sweat was pouring from his forehead, although it was a cool day. Fear stared out from his eyes. He was deadly serious.

Every feeling those with excessive energy have and every action they take is intensified by this inner push. It pushes, pushes, pushes, not in any certain direction, just pushes. This is what creates such a problem for the individual who is so infected. He must choose the direction. And the secret of whether it makes him a failure or success depends on his ability to control it and keep it headed in the right direction. It is like putting exceedingly high octane gasoline in a car. It will go, but there has to be a driver at the wheel.

The tendency is to become highly enthusiastic about a project, a job or a career. They throw their whole being, their energy, drive and ambition into it, and things begin to happen—because they can get results. After, about the time that the boss and their friends feel that he is a real find, he sees another opportunity and becomes just as excited about it. So he loses his enthusiasm about the first and starts off in a new direction. He just can't seem to finish anything. He is like the horseman who jumped on his horse and "rode off in all four directions."

Pete was just such a man. In the service he had climbed up to be a captain. He was intelligent, had a sparkling personality, was likeable, enthusiastic, loved people, generous and of course continually busy.

While in the service he felt that he should get out and become a salesman. "Know I can make a million," he told the other officers. And nobody laughed, because they thought he could, too.

His first job was on the floor in a furniture store. "Gotta learn the business," Pete told himself. He liked the fellows in the store, the "boss" and he loved talking to customers. Feeling that here was a man that he could make his number two man in a few years, the owner took pains to teach Pete as much as he could. His third month he led the sales force in sales. He wasn't content to talk to customers on the floor; he would follow up by going out to the house to finish the sale. He made a couple or three calls this way almost every night.

But Pete had his eye on the biggest store in town. "If I worked there, I'd have the merchandise, the customers and the prestige," he argued with himself. It was about the end of his fifth month in the furniture business that he dropped in to talk with Mr. Constant, president of this biggest store.

Pete went to the new job the first of the month. He was fired with enthusiasm. "Boy, this is it," he mumbled as he went to wait on his first customer.

He had been on his new job and doing very well for some three months when he met Jack. Jack was a traveling salesman who represented the factory which built the highest quality living room furniture. They had lunch together.

Pete got the job as well as a choice territory in the Southeast with headquarters in Atlanta. "This is the life," he thought. "No more being hemmed in by four walls—all of Georgia, Florida and Alabama, this is my world."

He did like the traveling, new faces, new places, activity, variety, change; these are what a man like Pete needs. At the end of his first year, the longest he had ever been on a job, he figured up his earnings. Far below the $35,000 he had anticipated, but he did gross $20,000. "But living room furniture moves so slow," he told himself. "One suite will last a family for years. If I had something that didn't last so long." So he began to look about.

His next job, a couple of months later was as assistant manager of a furniture store for a chain on the Eastern seaboard. He was "almost" promised a store of his own in a couple of years. Then he would make his $35,000 and with no traveling expenses to pay out of it.

But two years is a long time. Pete just couldn't wait. Then, too, he missed the variety of traveling. It was those "four walls" again, so he went back on the road for a floor covering manufacturer, one of the best in the business.

The last time we saw Pete he was 48 years old and on the floor of a small "bargain" furniture store, one that sold a household full of furniture for $3.09 down and $3.09 a week. He had reached his peak with the floor-covering company, made just over twenty-five thousand, but his expenses came out and left him about ten thousand. Personnel directors spotted him as a "job jumper" and wouldn't give him much of a chance. He had had some forty jobs. "How are you doing, Pete?" we asked. "Aw, there's not much chance with this crummy outfit. Their merchandise is no good. But I've got my application in down the street at Kaplan's, the exclusive furniture store. Now, there's a place where I can really do good."

It seems that the "high drive, energetic" people just have to have variety and change. Some can get it in their career without constant job-hopping, but this requires planning and, above all, self-control.

Others have been able to satisfy their personal needs and, at the same time, continue in the one direction by engaging in two jobs or occupations, at the same time. Another such individual has completed college and two years of graduate school. One man with a wife and four children went back to college at age 43 and received three degrees while running a business, and part of the time two businesses.

Men and women with this excessively high energetic level sometimes have to choose not one career or another, but one career *and* another. They are addicted to work—just can't help it. One such man quit a job because the boss insisted on his taking a vacation. It is not uncommon for one of these individuals to go for many years without a vacation. Others work seven days a week, putting in as many as eighty hours. Why do they do it? Simply because they can't help it. Rich or poor, the push inside them keeps pushing and shoving and the individual has to respond.

You can easily see how awful it is to be married to such a person—that is, unless you are just like him and can understand his problems and his motivations. You want to sleep late on a weekend morning and he insists on getting up at some ungodly hour. You come in late from a social affair, are tired and want to sleep for a week; he has an idea and wants to go to the office and work three or four hours. And if he is the lonesome type, he may want you to go with him. After you have had a hard day and are ready for a quiet evening with a book or TV and early to bed, he wants to go dancing. You plan to attend a social affair or have invited a friend in, and he suddenly decides he must drive across the state and see a man about a proposition.

Or even worse, just after you have assured your parents that Joe now has a job and is determined to stay with it, he walks in and says, "I've quit." You can see a few of the many marriage problems that are caused by a man who is afflicted with this high level of energy. Only one thing is worse for a marriage and that is a woman who has this high drive, married to a man who is normal. It is not something that you can squelch or dam up or ignore.

It is a blessing to the one who has enough self-control to exploit it and keep it driving in one direction. It is a curse to the man or woman who allows it to dominate his life and drive him like a jet bomber streaming through the heavens at the speed of sound, with full tanks, *and no pilot.*

Certainly, it must be remembered that any asset can also be a liability—every good trait also a bad trait. It is excellent when a child has the persistence that will allow him to stay with a task you give him until he finishes it. But he will also be just as persistent about driving the family car before he reaches the legal age. He will insist, beg, plead, try to outwit you until you nearly go crazy telling him "No." Yet he persists. Then, it is not a good trait. The child who always tells the truth will just as truthfully tell Uncle Ben, from whom you hope to inherit a fortune, that you think him an awful bore and a little nutty.

The woman who marries an ambitious, energetic, hard-working man can also expect that he will take an extra job, work overtime or start a second business just when she wants to go on a vacation, or will get up at six in the morning and expect his breakfast at 6:30 when she wants to sleep until 9:00.

Or when a man marries an intelligent woman, she will not only use this intelligence to help him solve some of his problems, but also to think up logical and good reasons why she should have what she wants and why he should not do what he so desperately desires to do.

When a dominant man, who likes to make all the decisions, marries a submissive woman who does not like to make them, he must accept the fact that she will helplessly call him when something goes wrong. He may be able to train her not to phone him at the office when the washing machine breaks down, but he will still have to make the arrangements to have it fixed.

Thus, every good trait has a bad side. In the selection of a mate, we have to accept one with the other. There is a degree of compromise possible. He can have his area and she hers. When both partners are highly dominant, for example, it is a good idea to discuss and determine areas of authority. Certain areas are his province, others are hers, and other decision-making areas are to be discussed between them.

The importance of one quality or another in your mate depends on you. No two individuals are alike in what they want or need. Even though several people will list the same qualities as desirable in an "ideal" mate, they will not put them in the same order of importance or to the same degree. And most of us do not consider the "bad" side of the traits. The man who wants a woman who will adequately take over in the time of an emergency, may object to her also taking over when there is not any emergency.

In the matter of energy, the man or woman with low energy level is content with fewer activities and most often seems to accomplish what he or she needs to get done. The highly energetic individual often complains that he never has time to get things done. Why is this? The human dynamo has a tendency to take on more projects than even he can accomplish. He often has half a dozen or more projects going at the same time. Though he accomplishes more than the average individual, there is always something that has not been finished and by the time he finishes that he has already started on something else. Because of this, he feels that he doesn't get things done.

It may be that the most comfortable mate is the one with average or a little lower energy. If a man, he will be satisfied to work his forty hours a week, then come home and spend the rest of the time with his family in low activity pursuits. He may not be so ambitious, may not even earn as much, but will have more home life. The same is true for the woman; she may not care about outside-the-home activities and be content to let her husband relax and laze about the home as much as he desires, even if the lawn does need mowing.

THE TEST

8

The Compatibility Test

Women never truly command, 'til they have given their promise to obey; and they are never in more danger of being made slaves, than when the men are at their feet.

George Farquhar

The tests used in this book have been developed, refined and used by the authors for several years. The authors have given over 90,000 psychological tests during this time. The tests have been used for selecting employees for companies, deciding promotions and choosing executives. They have also been given for physicians and psychiatrists for purposes of diagnoses of psychological problems and in marriage counseling. Many of the persons who have taken the tests have been watched for twenty years or longer, and others for shorter periods to validate the tests.

Presently in this country, the majority of large, progressive companies are using similar tests—and indeed, some of the same questions in evaluating their management personnel and applicants. Constant research is being conducted by psychologists, business consultants, clinicians and personnel directors to make tests more valid in predicting the behavior of individuals in situations in which they have not been before. And this is exactly what a marriage is: this man and this woman have not lived as man and wife before, and they themselves do not know how they will act. Even if they have been married to another, a remarriage creates a new situation.

Promises, such as "I'll always love you," "I'll always be kind to you," or "I'll never leave you" are worthless. One never knows how he or she will act under other circumstances. Tests are better predictors than lovers' promises. Then, too, there is a change of attitudes after marriage. Tests measure the deeply imbedded personality factors which motivate us to unthinking behavior. But a caution: "measurement techniques (tests) cannot be expected to make decisions for you; they can only present the facts and evidence more clearly."

Another function of these tests is to present evidence about yourself, which you do not suspect, and about the other person which he cannot possibly know. We are all prone to believe that the way we feel and what we can do is normal and are the way everyone else feels and what they can do. But a thing which is easy—or very difficult—may be just the opposite for another, even one that he loves. The authors have often asked patients and clients about their sex drive or intelligence. If it has not been measured before, the subject invariably answers, "I suppose I'm about average." The facts may be quite different.

The only valid measurement of any human characteristic is in comparison with others in your cultural group. If you are asked whether you are tall or short, you can only answer by comparing yourself with those about you. But if you were in a culture where those about you were pygmies—a little over three feet high—you would be called a "giant" or very tall. On the other hand, if placed in a culture where everyone else was eight feet tall, they would call you "shorty" even at your present height. Psychological tests do just this: they compare you with the other people in the population. Therefore, psychological tests can give you an appraisal of yourself as compared with others.

Because of this, tests can say that you have a high or low heterosexual need; can tell whether you are dominant or submissive; if you are emotionally stable or neurotic, as compared with others. Thus they will show how you compare in those characteristics which social workers, psychologists, psychiatrists, marriage counsellors and others who deal with marriage problems have found important in marriage compatibility. These are the bases of the test in this book. It has been found to be reliable in the measurement of these factors.

So far the discussion has been of the factors included in Compatibility-One. This has been to prepare you to take the Compatibility Test. This Test is designed for three categories of people:

1. Those who have *never been married.* It can be taken before or after finding the person whom you feel to be your ideal mate. If taken before, it will aid you in your search. If you have already found your intended, it will show you what problems you will have if the two of you marry.

2. For those who *have been married* and are either divorced or widowed and do not intend to remain single. Certainly you want your new marriage to be happy and successful. Having been married, you are acquainted with the many things which can happen to destroy a marriage, even one that began with prospects of "living happily ever afterwards." You want to be more careful in selecting a man or woman unto whom you are going to entrust your body, mind and happiness. This test is designed to give you every chance of finding

what you truly desire this time. You have to be extremely careful for you realize that a second marriage only has a fifty percent chance of succeeding, and a third marriage only one chance in ten; for a fourth or fifth marriage, there are no reliable statistics, but certainly it is far less than a third.

3. Those who are *now married and are having problems.* You are certain that the source of these difficulties is within the two of you and not in the fact of marriage itself. It may be that you are convinced that your incompatibilities are wholly in your mate, but, then, there are some uncertainties in your mind, aren't there? Both of you were sure before you said, "I do," that this was the right partner for you. Take the test now and see just where the difficulties lie. "Finding a problem is the first step in solving it." Then, too, if there are deficiencies in you and you divorce this mate, you will carry them into any future marriage.

If you do not find the problem in the basic compatibilities, the last two chapters of this book are written to help you make a better adjustment to your mate. If you do find basic incompatibilities, go back and read the chapters on the basic incompatibilities and see if you do not see some solution which will help you. This book is the result of a quarter of a century of clinical practice with marital problems. Go back, and perhaps the very solution you need is on a page that you skimmed.

If you still do not find it, seek help from a clinical psychologist, a psychiatrist or a marriage counsellor. You will find each of these listed in the yellow pages of your telephone book, or better yet, ask your family physician to refer you.

NOTE: Those employed professionally in one of the behavioral or social sciences may obtain a copy of the test's technical manual by sending $2.00 to:

Dr. C. M. Whipple
Department of Psychology
Central Oklahoma State University
Edmond, Oklahoma 73034

CAUTION

It is important that the two of you do NOT take the test at the same time or while together. Each should take it when *alone* and when and where you will not be disturbed. Do not discuss the questions or your answers before you both have completed the test. Do not look over the questions before you take it. And it is just as important *that you do* discuss them after you have each completed the test and scored it. Discussion of the questions will give you much insight into the thinking and feelings of the other. We repeat: do NOT read over the questions before you are ready to take the test. Then read each question a couple of times, or until you are sure you understand it, and mark your answer. Then the next question and so on. One other thing, be truthful, even if it is embarrassing to you; if you are not, you are storing up heartaches for yourself and for the one you love.

> *Never lose sight of this important truth, that no one can be truly great until he has gained a knowledge of himself.*
>
> **Johann George Zimmerman**

IF YOU CHEAT, YOU CHEAT ONLY YOURSELF

INSTRUCTIONS

This is a test measuring several factors which have to do with compatibility and selecting a person of the opposite sex with whom you can make an agreeable marriage. It has not been tested for a "same sex" marriage. There are no right or wrong answers, although each can be answered "Yes" or "No." You may find one or two where it is not easy to give a definite answer, but consider well before giving up; if you still cannot say definitely, answer with a question mark. *But do not use the question mark to avoid making a decision.* The more question marks, the less accurate the Test.

It is usually easier if you mark your first impression. Since the results will be important to you, give frank, honest and truthful answers. Do not answer as you think you *should* answer or try to outguess the Test. The Test is only as accurate as the information you give it. Put all of your answers on a separate sheet; make no marks in the book.

Example:	Yes	?	No
Would you prefer a mate who is pleasant?	X	o	o
Do you object to a mate who sings?	o	o	X

DO NOT ALLOW SOMEONE TO HELP YOU OR GIVE YOU ANSWERS!

THE MARRIAGE COMPATIBILITY INVENTORY

Charles M. Whipple, Jr. and Dick Whittle

BEGIN HERE:

1. Would you dislike work where you were completely alone for weeks even if the pay was exceptionally high?

2. Can you become so absorbed in creative work that you would not notice the absence of friends?

3. Does it make you impatient to have someone interrupt when working on something important?

4. Is sex relations before marriage allowable for a couple to determine their fitness for one another?

5. Have you ever had blank spells when your activities were interrupted and you did not know what was going on?

6. When a child, did you belong to a crowd or gang that tried to stick together through thick and thin?

7. Do you find some people so bossy you want to do the opposite even if you know they are right?

8. Have there been times when your mind raced so fast that afterwards you did not realize the details of what you had been doing?

9. Have you occasionally stood in the way of another who was trying to do something, not because it was important, but for the principle of the thing?

10. Have you ever had attacks when you could not control your movements or speech but knew what was going on?

11. Have you met problems so full of possibilities that you have been unable to make up your mind about them?

12. Have you ever had spells of laughing or crying you could not control?

13. Have you often had to take orders from someone who did not know as much as you?

14. Do you have such strong sex urges that they should be judged by different standards than others?

15. Do you often wonder if a particular person of the opposite sex would be a good "bed partner"?

16. Do you at times have a strong desire to do something harmful or shocking?

17. Does it make you uncomfortable to be "different" or unconventional?

18. Do you sometimes keep on at a thing until others lose their patience with you?

19. Do you become discouraged if opinions of others are different from yours?

20. Do you ever fuss when a repairman does not get your work done on time?

21. Do you get a feeling of delight when almost any person of the opposite sex touches you?

22. Is your speech the same as always, not faster, slower or slurring; no hoarseness?

23. Would it make you self-conscious to lead a discussion in a group meeting?

24. Do you seem to like children of the opposite sex more than those of the same sex as yourself?

25. Are you often unable to make up your mind until the time for action is past?

26. Do you find that telling others about your good luck is the greatest pleasure of it?

27. Would it make you nervous if one of your family got in trouble with the law?

28. Can you figure out a problem alone better than discussing it with others?

29. Does your mind wander so badly at times that you lose track of what you are doing?

30. Have you been inspired to a program of life based on duty, which you carefully follow?

31. Can you stick to a boring job for a long time without encouragement or being driven?

32. Are you disgusted with the law when a criminal is freed by a smart lawyer?

33. Do you blame a person for taking advantage of one who lays himself open to it?

34. Do you resent a person of the opposite sex touching your hands, arms or shoulders?

35. Are you irritable and nervous without sex relations two or more times a month?

36. If several people get into trouble, should they agree on a story and stick to it?

37. Are you willing to take a chance alone in a situation of doubtful outcome?

38. Do you occasionally need stimulation by contact with successful people?

39. Do your feelings go from happiness to sadness without apparent reason?

40. Is it hard to ask for favors even if you are not sure you can return them?

41. At a gathering are you hesitant to meet the most important person there?

42. Do some of your family have habits which annoy or bother you very much?

43. Are there times when you can make up your mind with unusual ease?

44. Do you get as many ideas from books as from discussion with others?

45. Do you blame anyone for trying to grab anything he can get in this world?

46. Are you careful not to say something that will hurt another's feelings?

47. Are you embarrassed if you greet a stranger, thinking it to be a friend?

48. Do you find it hard to start a conversation when you meet new people?

49. Should one try to understand his dreams and be guided by them?

50. Have you ever tried to bluff your way past a doorman or guard?

51. A man is always (?) than his son: (1) taller; (2) wiser; (3) older

52. There was a man and his wife, three sons and their wives, and four children in each son's family. How many altogether? (1) 20; (2) 18; (3) 12

53. A church is most likely to have: (1) minister; (2) choir; (3) congregation

54. If a movie camera takes 6 pictures in ¼ second, how many will it take in 10 seconds? (1) 24; (2) 60; (3) 240

55. What letter is the third letter to the left of the letter that is midway between D and A in the word INDIGNATION? (1) T; (2) N; (3) G

56. If the words NAN, NON, DAD, PEP, and TOT were seen in a mirror, how many would appear exactly as if seen directly? (1) 1; (2) 3; (3) 4

57. If it takes two (2) pints of cream and three (3) pints of milk

mixed to make coffee cream, how much milk is needed to make $2\frac{1}{2}$ gallons of coffee cream? (1) 12 pints; (2) 10 pints; (3) 6 pints

58. Sam is older than Carl, Tom is older than Sam, Carl is younger than Tom. If the first two statements are true, the third is—(1) true; (2) uncertain; (3) false

59. How would you best judge a man's character? By his—(1) looks; (2) behavior; (3) religious belief

60. The opposite of natural is—(1) strange; (2) foreign; (3) artificial

61. Which letter group is different? (1) EMLKE; (2) AGFKA; (3) UQPKU

62. Everyone in the club is rich. Fred does not belong to the club. Fred is not rich. If the first two statements are true, the third is—(1) true; (2) uncertain; (3) false

63. If all the even numbered letters in the alphabet were removed, the eighth letter remaining would be—(1) H; (2) O; (3) P

64. I like to feel smooth, gooey and soft things.

65. Do you worry over bad things which may happen?

66. Should women have as much sexual freedom as men?

67. Is it true that you never worry about your looks?

68. Would you rather make a quick decision alone?

69. Is kissing parts of the body other than the face exciting?

70. Do you like to have your back and arms rubbed?

71. Are there subjects that bother you to talk about?

72. Are you timid around people of special importance?

73. Should kissing on the lips be avoided because of germs?

74. Are you kept awake by ideas running through your head?

75. Do you like to pet children, even if they are strangers?

76. Do you dread taking back articles you have bought?

77. Do you know who is responsible for most of your troubles?

78. In marriage, sex play should be confined to late evening.

79. Does it bother you for someone to watch you while you work?

80. Do you daydream a great deal about love and romance?

81. Are good books more entertaining than people?

82. Do you like to take on added responsibilities?

83. Would you prefer a modern dance step to a waltz?

84. Should a woman choose death rather than be raped?

85. Are you very talkative at social gatherings?

86. Do you usually work under a great deal of tension?

87. Have you at times wanted to leave home very badly?

88. Do you dislike finding your way about in strange places?
89. Are athletics more interesting than intellectual affairs?
90. Do you enjoy social gatherings more than being alone?
91. Should intercourse only be used for producing children?
92. Do you get along better with people of the opposite sex?
93. Does a "nice" woman enjoy sexual contact?
94. Have you ever solicited funds or sold tickets?
95. Have you ever organized a club or group of your own?
96. Do you feel that you are an important person?
97. Is talking more helpful in making a decision than reading?
98. Do you find yourself strongly attracted to those of the opposite sex?
99. Can you stand criticism without feeling hurt?
100. Do normal people sometimes indulge in unusual sex practices?
101. Are things funnier to you if you are with others than if alone?
102. Do you have difficulty starting a conversation with a stranger?
103. In a restaurant do you ever complain if the food is not good?
104. If a woman is being raped, should she fight until knocked out?
105. Have you ever done anything dangerous just for the thrill of it?
106. Are your table manners as good at home as when in company?
107. Do your thoughts race ahead at times faster than you can speak them?
108. When happy, elated or sad, do you keep your feelings to yourself?
109. Do you get so restless at times it is hard to sit long in a chair?
110. Should sex perverts be imprisoned?
111. Do you usually face troubles alone without seeking help?
112. Are you strongly attracted by people of the opposite sex?
113. Have your strong sex urges gotten you into tight places?
114. Do you have trouble making up your mind for yourself?
115. Do you feel that people on the street are watching you?
116. Are people more stimulating to you than anything else?
117. Is it hard for your relatives to realize that you have grown up?
118. Do you want the opinions of others to help make a decision?
119. Do you like to introduce people at a gathering or a party?
120. Can you usually make better plans alone than with others helping?
121. Do you feel that you have often been punished without cause?
122. Is being kissed elsewhere on the body than the face exciting?

123. Do useless thoughts keep coming into your mind over and over?
124. Do you try to stir up some excitement when you get bored?
125. Are you able to play your best against a superior opponent?
126. Is observation of social customs and manners essential?
127. Do you try to find someone to cheer you when in low spirits?
128. Do you drink an unusually large amount of water everyday?
129. Is a married person justified in killing a mate caught in adultery?
130. Do you like to stay in the background at social gatherings?
131. Will excitement pull you out of it when you are feeling low?
132. Are you considered to be indifferent to the opposite sex?
133. Can you be happy when those about you are depressed?
134. Do you become quite excited at least once a week?
135. Do you sweat very easily even on cool days?
136. Is marriage necessary for your happiness?
137. Would you attend a sexy show if you could avoid it?
138. Do you want to be with people when you have tough luck?
139. Do you make many small errors in your work?
140. Do you have trouble believing what the church teaches?
141. Does it give you fear to look down from a high place?
142. Do you have some fear of people of the opposite sex?
143. Do you have many pleasant and unpleasant moods?
144. Does admiration gratify you more than achievement?
145. Do you wish you were not bothered by thoughts of sex?
146. Do people sometimes take advantage of you?
147. Are you bothered by feelings of inferiority?
148. Do you consider yourself very affectionate?
149. Should children be taught all the main facts of sex?
150. In clothes, do you prefer soft clothes to durable ones?
151. Would you rather go fishing than to a ball game?
152. Do you want to be alone in times of bad luck?
153. "Spade" is to "dig" as "knife" is to: (1) sharp; (2) cut; (3) shovel
154. "Tired" is to "work" as "proud" is to: (1) rest; (2) success; (3) exercise
155. "Surprise" is to "strange" as "fear" is to: (1) brave; (2) anxious; (3) terrible
156. Which of these fractions is the "different" one? (1) $3/7$; (2) $3/9$; (3) $3/11$
157. "Size" is to "length" as "dishonesty" is to: (1) prison; (2) sin; (3) stealing

158. "AB" is to "dc" as "SR" is to: (1) qp; (2) pq; (3) tu
159. "Better" is to "worst" as "slower" is to: (1) fast; (2) best; (3) quickest
160. Which of these words does not belong with the others? (1) any; (2) some; (3) most
161. Which of these is different in kind from the others? (1) candle; (2) moon; (3) electric light
162. "Flame" is to "heat" as "rose" is to: (1) thorn; (2) red petals; (3) scent
163. Which of these words does not belong with the others? (1) wide; (2) zigzag; (3) regular
164. "Soon" is to "never" as "near" is to: (1) nowhere; (2) far; (3) next
165. The different one: (1) pen; (2) chalk; (3) paper
166. An auto is most likely to have: (1) spare tire; (2) gas tank; (3) fenders
167. Do you worry a long time if humiliated?
168. Do you ever question a public speaker?
169. Do people ever come to you for advice?
170. Do you prefer to be around younger people?
171. Do you like to bear responsibility alone?
172. Have you ever had spells of dizziness?
173. Is one of your favorite colors warm red?
174. Do you like to lie in a warm bath and enjoy the feelings?
175. Is sex a very important part of life to you?
176. Do you enjoy spending an evening alone?
177. Does discipline make you unhappy?
178. Do you like to be with others very much?
179. Do you need a great deal of affection?
180. Do you often feel lonesome in a crowd?
181. Did you like kissing games as a child?
182. Do you ever give money to beggars?
183. Is it easy for you to make new friends?
184. Is it hard to get rid of a salesman?
185. Do you sometimes dream of snakes?
186. Would you prefer a play to a dance?
187. Would you prefer to work with others?
188. Do people think you critical of others?
189. Do you try to liven up a dead party?

190. Are you slow in making decisions?
191. Do you get stage fright if up before people?
192. Do you prefer a double bed to twin beds?
193. Is it easy to get your feelings hurt?
194. Is it hard for you to speak in public?
195. Do you like many visitors when ill?
196. Do you daydream frequently?
197. Are you fascinated by fire?
198. Do you lack self-confidence?
199. Do you love to go to dances?
200. Do you like to talk about sex?
201. Do you often feel grouchy?
202. Are you a nervous person?
203. Do you blush often?
204. Are you shy at times?
205. Do you often get lonely?
206. Do you cry often?
207. Do you like to flirt?
208. Do you enjoy children?

9

How to Score the Test

Surely, after you have completed the test, you are anxious to know the results, and you can in just a few minutes. The scoring has been simplified to give you as little bother as possible. Your learning the results involves only four steps:

1. Turn to the back of the book to the section entitled "correct answers." Compare your responses, number by number, with the correct answers. You then write your total count (the number of your responses that matched the correct answers) for that factor at the bottom in the space provided for that score. Do all the factors the same way. You will now have six scores for A, B, C, D, E, and F.

2. Next, turn to the section entitled Code Conversion Chart, Male and Female. If you are a man and your score on Factor A is 45, for instance, trace with your finger to the extreme left, and you will note that this is equal to an interpretation rating of 1. This is the score that is used for matching. If the score on Factor A had been 31, on the other hand, the 31 would be equal to an interpretation rating of 3.

3. Using this interpretation rating of, say, 3, one could look at the matching chart and see what rating one would look for in a mate. If the score of 3 is on the male, the chart suggests he can make the best adjustment with a female with either a 3 or a 4 rating, as seen in the third column in Factor A. If a score of 3 is obtained by a female, she will mate best with a man who has either a 2 or a 3 rating, as seen in the second and third columns for the left. Other factors, of course, are done in the same way.

4. To obtain a write-up on yourself for this factor, turn to "write-ups male" or "write-ups female" and find paragraph A-3. This can be cut out of the book, cutting on the dotted line, and pasted on a sheet of paper. Proceed the same way for factors B, C, D, E, and F.

10

Interpretation—Male

INSTRUCTIONS: From your scoring you have an interpretation rating of either 1, 2, 3, 4, or 5 for each of the factors, A, B, C, D, E, and F. By combining these, you will have the keys to these write-ups. If, for instance, the score is 1 on factor A, the write-up will be that appearing opposite A-1 below. If the score is 3 on factor A, it will appear opposite A-3. The same holds true for all of the other factors.

To have a complete Compatibility write-up *on the person taking the test,* one only needs to cut out the write-up for each combined key (such as A-3, B-2, C-4, D-2, E-1, F-5) and paste them on sheets of paper. These are printed only on one side of the paper to allow for this. The write up for the female can be done the same way. Then the write-ups can be compared factor for factor (male A to female A, male B to female B, etc.).

For those who are not married at the time of taking the test, if there are incompatibilities (ratings which did not match on the Matching Chart), it is suggested that you re-read the chapter on that factor, as shown below, and understand the risk you are taking and what, if anything, can be done about it.

Factor A - Sociability
Factor B - Emotional Stability
Factor C - Dominance
Factor D Intellectual and Educational Level
Factor E - Heterosexual Need
Factor F - Drive Level

CAUTION: If there are two or more incompatibilities shown, expect trouble in the marriage. More than three is an almost impossible situation. Remember, neither this nor any other test by itself can give a complete or totally accurate picture of personality functioning. This test, at best, serves as an objective device to assist you in the screening of possible marriage partners or show areas of functioning which you and your loved one can build on or attempt to correct. It is strongly suggested, in your attempts to correct any such weaknesses, that you avail yourself of professional help. In many instances, this will involve further testing.

- -Cut on this line- -

FACTOR A

A-1. You like people—crowds—and don't want to be by yourself. In your selection of a mate, be sure that you pick one who is a goer and not one who wants to stay at home. While dating you should watch to see if she likes to go places where there are other people: games rather than a picnic, a party rather than fishing. And she should not let herself be tied down to responsibilities when you want to go. A tip: a goer can get ready on a moment's notice.

- -Cut on this line- -

A-2. You need people around you a good deal of the time. You will do best with a girl friend or wife who is sociable and a good mixer. She should like to be with people most of the time but not all the time. The girl who says she is a "home maker" is often a stay-home girl. Give a girl a call thirty minutes before leaving for a party or a trip. A goer will be ready.

- -Cut on this line- -

A-3. You like about an even mixture of quietude and parties. Contact with others stimulates you but can get on your nerves if it becomes constant. Unless your vocation gives you enough "socializing," do not tie yourself to one who likes to sit at home most of the time. This will seem relatively unimportant during courtship but things change after marriage. Many men think their wives have changed when actually they have only begun the regular routine, which was predicted before marriage by their behavior.

- -Cut on this line- -

A-4. Some women want to be on the go all the time and never want to spend an evening alone, even with their man. Avoid such women. They are not for you. You want the quietness and solitude of time away from the mob. Find yourself a girl who is the same way and can enjoy simple pleasures.

- -Cut on this line- -

- -Cut on this line- -

A-5. Quiet people like quiet people. Those who dislike mobs, heavy traffic and crowds. You are such an individual. Find yourself a girl who is the same way. Such a woman can be happy working and playing alone or with only one companion.

- -Cut on this line- -

FACTOR B

B-1. Since you are a stable, secure, well-adjusted individual, you will need a woman who is just as well-adjusted as you. Look for symptoms of instability during the time you are dating. It is suggested that you read the chapter on Emotional Stability again before marrying any other type of woman.

- -Cut on this line- -

B-2. You are emotionally more stable than the average man although you still exhibit some weaknesses and, at times, are a little uncertain about your masculinity. It will be advisable, then, not to have a neurotic girl friend or wife. Determining how a woman thinks her family feels toward her will be a cue as to how she will feel toward you.

- -Cut on this line- -

B-3. You occasionally have trouble in feeling secure and self-confident. Find a wife who can support you emotionally when you need it and who, at the same time, needs your support in areas in which she feels insecure. It will help if you find a woman who admires you in addition to being in love with you.

- -Cut on this line- -

- -Cut on this line- -

B-4 & 5. You badly need warmth and affection around you, yet you never seem to have had it. This is one of your secrets. It seems that no matter how hard you have tried, or what you have done, you have not gotten the needed love from your family, friends or even a mate. Other people like you much better than you like yourself. You are unhappy and no woman can, by herself, make you happy. You can make a better adjustment with a woman who compensates for your weaknesses but she must also be able to benefit from your strengths.

- -Cut on this line- -

FACTOR C

C-1. Your extremely strong personality makes you a dominant male. You tend to overpower others with your personality. This is an excellent trait in many vocations which require leadership, supervision and some types of selling. There is a danger in marriage of you becoming too dominating, inconsiderate of the feelings of your wife, and certainly too possessive. Study the principles of democratic leadership, and it will benefit you in your relations both on the job and in the home.

- -Cut on this line- -

C-2. You are stronger in personality than the average man. You can, at times, be "bullheaded" but most of the time you are willing to listen to and consider the other person's point of view. Most people tend to let you lead. Your ability to compromise will allow you to make a much better adjustment to family and work, especially if your wife has the same strengths and willingness to compromise.

- -Cut on this line- -

- -Cut on this line- -

C-3. You are an easy going individual who can both give and take orders. In your selection of a girl friend or wife beware of the dominating woman who will try to put a man under her thumb after marriage. Your ideal marital partner will be just that—a partner. She should neither dominate you or you her. Decision making should be a joint enterprise with a firm prior agreement as to who has the last word in those areas in which you cannot come to an agreement. Such a division of responsibility will make the home run much more smoothly and keep arguments to the minimum—if you stick to it.

- -Cut on this line- -

C-4. You don't like to argue. You would prefer to do what the other person wants rather than get into a hassle over the issue. But when you select a mate, be sure that she is not dominating or bossy. You will grow to resent such disregard of your thoughts and feelings. You will do much better to plan your home life and decide just what both of you want. You can then let her implement the minor points of your plan without fear of her domination or your being trampled on. A quarterly review of your plan, at a time when you are both in a good mood, will keep it up to date and diminish arguments.

- -Cut on this line- -

C-5. You are inclined to push off too many decisions for the woman to make. If this is continued, she will become bossy and take over, making all decisions. For your own protection you should learn more about decision making and train yourself to be more assertive of your rights. Books from the business area on how to plan and make decisions will be very beneficial to you and help in creating a more equal home life.

- -Cut on this line- -

-----------------------Cut on this line--------------------

FACTOR D

D-1. You are cursed with brains. By this is meant that you have more intelligence than most of the people in this country.

In the selection of a mate, you will want a girl who can appreciate your talents, urge you to find and use them and inspire you to take advantage of these capacities to their fullest. She need not be as intelligent as you, but she should not be far below or you will grow to be ashamed of her and possibly wreck your marriage. You probably will want a girl who will be able to talk on your level, think as fast as you, or at least follow you, and of whom you can be proud. Do not think that beauty or charm can compensate for low intelligence. They cannot.

-----------------------Cut on this line--------------------

D-2. Since you are more intelligent than the average man, you will be required to get more training and education than the average man.

In selecting a mate, choose one who can help you exploit your talents and achieve your goals. She should be smart and able to think. The ideas she can produce, when combined with those you have, can push you twice as fast and bring more happiness to both of you. By the way, if you have not found out where your talents lie, Aptitude Tests can show you. See a psychologist.

-----------------------Cut on this line--------------------

D-3. Those who are far-sighted enough to be concerned about choosing the right *mate instead of just looking for a pretty face and striking figure are above average in intelligence, among other things. This places upon you, as one of them, the responsibility of recognizing and using this mentality. If you do not train and educate this intelligence, then get into a vocation which demands its use, you will be an unhappy man. Shy away from the so-called brainy woman who tries to mentally dominate her man. Beware, this means trouble—unless you will go to school and become "smarter."*

-----------------------Cut on this line--------------------

------------------------Cut on this line------------------------

D-4. You are fortunate in that you are intellectually fitted to fill three-fourths of the more than 90,000 jobs by which Americans make a living. For a woman to look up to and respect you, you should be smarter and as well educated as she; therefore pass up the so-called brainy women in favor of the more realistic, down-to-earth women. The woman who prides herself in her intellectual achievement will not bring you happiness.

------------------------Cut on this line------------------------

D-5. You are not an "egg head" or one of the "intelligentsia," but you are an unusual man, or you wouldn't be reading this. You are one of the men about whom the world turns. You and men like you perform most of the world's work and possess most of the skills. In selecting your woman, you want a very practical woman who has realistic notions of life and does not expect a man to give her fur coats and the moon. Seek a modest woman who takes pride in being a woman and giving companionship and love to her man. You need emotional satisfaction and not intellectual prodding and nagging.

------------------------Cut on this line------------------------

FACTOR E

E-1. You are a man who has very high heterosexual needs and are not likely to be satisfied with the average woman. After a short while you will develop a feeling that you are being rejected and this is detrimental to a marriage. Only a small percentage of women, about 10%, will have the warmth and affection you require; but, of course there are many such women. Depending on your background, you may be attracted to female "sexpots." This may be a mistake, as discussed in this book. Women are drawn to you even though they do not realize why. You will live intensely and can be as happy as an angel or as miserable as a devil in hell.

------------------------Cut on this line------------------------

- -Cut on this line- -

E-2. Women feel an attraction toward you, even when their conventionality and up-bringing prevents their showing it. But there are more women who will be mismatches for you than will be compatible. It is imperative that before you become serious with any *woman that a Compatibility Test be run on her. It is important that you find one who will be equal to you in warmth and affection. There are many such women, probably 25-30% of the women.*

- -Cut on this line- -

E-3. You are one of the luckiest of all men. You measure in this area where most of the women are found. There are women who are cold and calculating and others who are overly sensual and passionate. You want neither of these. Either will lead you into unhappiness and misery. It is natural for a man to be attracted to women whose beautifully formed bodies, carnal walk and voluptuous face promise much. But a few years and a few calories will change these all too soon. You will be wise in your selection of a woman if attracted by other more important qualities—those which will last through the years.

- -Cut on this line- -

E-4. Your emotional adjustments are such that most women are compatible with you. But, of course, the law doesn't allow you to marry most women—only one. And there are many in this country who are built exactly to suit you. And they are not suited for most men either, only those with the unique make-up you possess. But, you will need to use care in selecting a woman to date or to marry. You certainly will not want a woman who wishes to spend most of her life in bed. Therefore shy away from those who are filled with romantic dreams, are mushy in their affection and have a compulsion to get married right away. Shy away also from the sexy girl; she can only bring unhappiness and heartache to you.

- -Cut on this line- -

- -Cut on this line- -

E-5. Select a woman who is more interested in doing things other than petting and mumbling sweet nothings; one who expresses love through actions rather than just words; one who can help you to accomplish your goals and build a life on the more important aspects of companionship instead of just love. This is normal—normal for you and her. Reject the idea of many men that man only expresses his manhood and virility through sexual exploits. It is a myth and not true. Nature has blessed you in building you so that there are many things you want and desire more than sexual love–and this is right and good.

- -Cut on this line- -

FACTOR F

F-1. You want to always be on the go, doing things, seeing new places, having excitement, hurry, fast traffic, contests, sports, muscular activity and you even talk and think fast. These are excellent qualities, but only if you can control all of this energy and keep it headed in one direction. Really, you want to go in several directions at once, thus you are liable to become a job jumper and irresponsible. Now in looking for a woman who can keep up with you, get one that has as much energy and drive as you. Of all things, don't marry a lazy one.

- -Cut on this line- -

F-2. You have an inner push and ambition. It's even hard for you to sit down and talk—much harder to read a book. This is fine in the business world because almost all of those who get ahead and climb in companies have this same drive. But whether you climb will depend on your ability to curb your tendency to always be looking for greener pastures elsewhere. Socially and matrimonially you will need a girl with as much energy as you; do not choose a stay-at-home girl who tires easily or you will tire of her.

- -Cut on this line- -

- -Cut on this line- -

F-3. One of your assets can pay you big dividends. You have more energy than the average man—this is push, use it. But a caution, it can make you either a job jumper or a man who gets ahead in life. Planning and setting long range objectives (5 years) and short range goals are helpful. If you are to seriously plan your life and set goals for yourself, it will help if you find a woman who can truly accept such goals, one who is as energetic as you.

- -Cut on this line- -

F-4. Life comes to you a day at a time and so you live it. You are realistic and know that "Rome wasn't built in a day." Also you know that there are so many things you want that there are some of them you can't get, so why fret. Find a woman who has the same ideas and not one who is a social climber or who wants the whole world. Get a woman who will be satisfied with you, and you her.

- -Cut on this line- -

F-5. You want to enjoy life. You don't want to be pushed or nagged by anyone. Beware of the overly ambitious woman who is always wanting something. You are more concerned with living each day as it comes along. And you need a woman who takes things easy and sees the beauty of life a day at a time. She will not give you many disappointments.

- -Cut on this line- -

11

Interpretation—Female

INSTRUCTIONS: You have now scored your test answers and have marked your profile chart. From this you have obtained your interpretation ratings of either 1, 2, 3, 4, or 5 for each factor. By combining this rating with the letter at the top of the columns on the Profile, you will have a key of A-1, A-2, A-3, A-4, or A-5, and the same for each of the other factors.

So that you may have a complete personality write-up on yourself or another female taking this Test, you will only need to cut out the write-up for each of these keys that apply to that person, and paste them on sheets of stationery. This part of the book is only printed on one side of the paper to allow this. The write-up for the male is done in the same way. The two write-ups can then be compared factor for factor. For those who are not married, the matching chart is used to determine the kind of mate which matches best. For those who are married, note any discrepancies in suitabilities. Go back and re-read the chapters covering these incompatibilities. Later in this book are two chapters on adjusting to differences in a mate. Those who are not married, if you find incompatibilities with your intended, you can now know what risks you are taking and what, if anything, can be done about it. The chapters covering the compatibility factors are:

Factor A - Sociability

Factor B - Emotional Stability

Factor C - Dominance

Factor D - Intellectual and Educational Level

Factor E - Heterosexual Need

Factor F - Drive Level

CAUTION: Go slow about marrying any man with incompatibilities that are shown up. Seek professional advice first. If three or more appear, better look elsewhere, you may have an impossible situation. Of course, if you are over 70, go ahead; you won't have to endure it long.

Remember, neither this nor any other test by itself can give a complete or totally accurate picture of personality functioning. This test, at best, purports to serve as an objective device to assist you in the screening of possible marriage partners or show areas of functioning which you and your loved one can build on or attempt to correct. It is strongly suggested, in your attempts to correct any such weaknesses, that you avail yourself of professional help. In many instances, this will involve further testing.

-----------------------Cut on this line-----------------------

FACTOR A

A-1. You like people—even more, love them. You nearly always want to be in a crowd, excitement, activity, laughter, loud noise; these things are your life. And it is not a bad trait. It brings happiness to you and will continue to do so, if—and this is a big if—you do not marry a man who does not like these things. A woman with as much need for people as you should be in a job where she is constantly with others: in the theatre, sports, politics, sales, teaching, and such occupations. Then she should have a man who is very people-loving as shown on the Matching Chart.

-----------------------Cut on this line-----------------------

A-2. You like people. You want to share your joys and sorrows with them and have them do the same with you. Be careful, therefore, in your selection of a mate. Remember a man may appear sociable just to be with you. But if you marry, he is likely to sit down. Since you get so much pleasure from people, do not deny yourself this enjoyment.

-----------------------Cut on this line-----------------------

A-3. The tests indicate that you are like about half of the people in the world—you like people, at least, more than the average woman. You will be more contented if, in selecting your man, you pick one who is as gregarious as you. You'll probably find him where people are and not on the bank of a lake fishing; so, go where groups gather and associate with sociable people.

-----------------------Cut on this line-----------------------

A-4. Now, you really don't like people around you all of the time. You need some time to yourself. You will, therefore, fit into a job where your contact with others is limited. Be sure your mate is a man who can enjoy staying at home without being bored, and be sure you *find it interesting being alone with him.*

-----------------------Cut on this line-----------------------

-----------------------Cut on this line-----------------------

A-5. In choosing an occupation, you should select one which will not put you in direct contact with people. Accounting or bookkeeping are both good, as are researcher, chemist, engraver, underwriter, programmer, copywriter, artist, and other of the more isolated types of jobs. You are the type of person who must have some time to herself. In the selection of a mate, you should definitely select a man who likes to be alone, or only with you, most of the time. Do not make the mistake of thinking that opposites attract in this area.

-----------------------Cut on this line-----------------------

FACTOR B

B-1. To one as stable as you, a sickly, pouty man, who is always getting his feelings hurt and venting emotional wrath and temper tantrums, is both disgusting and to be avoided. So observe the Matching Chart carefully to be sure you have a mate who is as stable emotionally as you are.

-----------------------Cut on this line-----------------------

B-2. You have been concerned because some of your friends and acquaintances are so unpredictable. You never know what to expect from them. Why is this? It is because they are not as emotionally secure as you. Do not have a man like this for a friend for you may marry him.

-----------------------Cut on this line-----------------------

B-3. You have difficulty sometimes because of insecurity and not being sure of yourself. But it is not all the time. At such times you need a strong man to lean upon, but positively not a neurotic one. Remember this in selecting a man with whom you are going to cast your lot.

-----------------------Cut on this line-----------------------

- -Cut on this line- -

B-4. It is important that you do not select a sadistic man. You punish yourself too much without having a man who enjoys hurting. You are a much finer person than you give yourself credit for being and can be liked and loved, if you will only allow it.

- -Cut on this line- -

B-5. Everyone about you likes you better than you do yourself—they always have. Your attitude of self-depreciation creates guilt feelings, even for little unimportant things, even things you think you might do. These things being true, find a man who is stronger and more secure than you, one you can lean upon, trust him, love him and depend on him.

- -Cut on this line- -

FACTOR C

C-1. You have an extremely strong personality. Too strong for most men. Therefore, it will require a very strong masterful man to hold your respect and love. Do not make the mistake that some strong women have and marry a mousey individual hoping to make him more aggressive. If you succeeded, he would hate you for it. You do face something of a conflict within yourself: when you are with a man you tend to dominate him. If you can, you will soon lose respect for him and be unhappy. If you find yourself doing this, either find a stronger man or control yourself.

- -Cut on this line- -

- -Cut on this line- -

C-2. Nature has made you a unique woman. You recognize that some men are weak and others strong. If you marry a weak man, it will distress both of you. Even if he begs you to marry him, shun him; he will only grow to hate you and you him. Be suspicious of men who, when they ask for a date, say, "anything you want to do." He's not being nice, he's probably just too weak to decide.

- -Cut on this line- -

C-3. You do not want to get into a marriage situation where you will have to make all the decisions. You therefore want a man who can make decisions and knows where he is going in life. Avoid a man who forces you to make the decisions on dates. A weak man cannot be leaned upon so look closely at the Matching Chart for compatibility in this factor.

- -Cut on this line- -

C-4. It's true that you don't like to make decisions nor assume all the responsibility. It's also true that you want the man to do these things. Do not go to extremes however. You do not want to marry a highly dominating male. You will do best in a partnership situation when your desires are brought out and discussed as well as his. When the two of you arrive at a joint decision, he will then be able to implement that decision for both of you.

- -Cut on this line- -

C-5. If you continue to push off decisions to the men, do not be surprised if you become one's servant. But, of course, you may enjoy that. Many women and not just a few men, prefer to be "slaves" of a strong master who will tell them what to do and take care of them. And this is well and good, if the chains are made of love. It is best if your man is strong enough for you to look up to and be proud of and yet who is kind and considerate and shows respect for you.

- -Cut on this line- -

- -Cut on this line- -

FACTOR D

D-1. There are indications that you are highly intelligent. This can either be a curse or a blessing, depending on what you do with it. In order for you to be happy, you must do at least two things: you absolutely must do some kind of work which will give you a mental challenge and, if you marry, you must get a man you can respect. Marry a brainy one—not just one who says he is. Marriage may not end your work career as your intelligence will require more challenge than you can get from a broom or dish cloth.

- -Cut on this line- -

D-2. Being a smart girl you should aspire to a higher intellectual type of man than most girls. But you will then have to keep up with him. Select your man from among the professional and businessmen who think. Get one who will be proud of your mind and not afraid of it. Then keep up with him through day or evening school and by studying. Mental activity and learning can bring you satisfaction.

- -Cut on this line- -

D-3. You are not particularly interested in purely mental things—you are more realistic and practical. Select your friends and husband from among people like yourself. You will like the things that most people like to do—and you can learn to do them well. This will give you satisfaction and a feeling of importance, of achievement and satisfaction.

- -Cut on this line- -

-----------------------Cut on this line-----------------------

D-4. You are what most men would term the ideal mate, at least mentally—not too brilliant so that you make them uncomfortable and not too dumb to excite their interest. You really do not care enough for intellectual things to embarrass men with a show of superior knowledge. You like men upon whose shoulders the work and accomplishment rest. But remember your man wants most from you the love and understanding which only you can give.

-----------------------Cut on this line-----------------------

D-5. There is a truthful old saying that "men do not want a brainy woman." Therefore, it will not become you to make a show of your knowledge and wisdom. A woman's intuition will tell you to be curious, the type who wants to know everything about her man—and others, too. You will be happiest with those men who match you on the Compatibility Test—and there are millions of them.

-----------------------Cut on this line-----------------------

FACTOR E

E-1. The Test indicates that you are a woman with extremely high emotional drives and needs. You will find that the most important thing in your life is companionship and the need for physical and emotional love. You should marry a man who is very warm and loving; that is, if you are to be happy. While this is not the only factor which is important, without compatibility here, the others will be distorted and thrown off kilter.

-----------------------Cut on this line-----------------------

- -Cut on this line- -

E-2. Within yourself you are broadminded and strongly attracted to men, and there is a reason. Your strong need for affection and love can cause you to make a mistake in choosing a mate. You will be in too much of a hurry. However, don't sit and wait for your man to come along. Go out and look for one who is especially tender, thoughtful, and thinks more of your happiness than his own. It's the little things which count with you, look for a man who does them.

- -Cut on this line- -

E-3. There are men who are cold, calculating and businesslike, others who are passionate and overpowering. Pass them both up. To select either will be a poor choice for you and will lead to marital unhappiness. Between these two extremes are the millions of men who will appreciate a woman such as you. Look for a man who has regard for your feelings. You will be happier.

- -Cut on this line- -

E-4. You are more idealistic and more interested in other things which are more important to you than running after a man and sex. Certainly you want your own man and home. But you must find a man who wants to be with a woman who is personally interesting, has something more than a body, and is a good companion instead of trying to appear to be a passionate sexpot. You will want a man who has the same interests as yours. To be your guy, he will pass up the fireballs and search out a realistic, practical, down-to-earth woman such as you.

- -Cut on this line- -

E-5. Due to your unique make-up, only a small percentage of the men can make you happy. For you, not just any man will do. Less than a fourth of them are right for you in this factor. Certainly you should not take a chance of marriage without a Compatibility Test on him and careful matching. Shy away from men with roaming hands, mushy words, those trying to get you to prove you're alive; these will bring you only misery. The right man will respect you and love not only your body but also your mind and heart.

- -Cut on this line- -

- -Cut on this line- -

FACTOR F

F-1. You have an excess of energy and are either cursed with it or blessed. This makes you want and even more feel a compulsion toward constant activity. To be satisfied, therefore, it will be necessary for you to find a man who constantly will be on the go and doing things. If you find a man like this, you can find excitement and variety; but beware of the man who tires easily, wants to sit a lot and who likes to stay home or you will be drowned in boredom.

- -Cut on this line- -

F-2. Down deep somewhere within you there is a force which just keeps pushing you. Therefore in selecting a man, if you are not to live a life of melancholy boredom, find a man who has this same push. This desire to always be doing something, going somewhere, activity, excitement, always moving, never tiring—what a match you two will make.

- -Cut on this line- -

F-3. You will never be able to carry out all your plans, do all the things you want to do, see all the sights, go to all the places. How wonderful if you did not have to waste time sleeping and doing the humdrum things of life, then you could experience more. This is symptomatic of your need for change and variety in life. And, of course, you must find a man who is the same way if you would have a happy marriage.

- -Cut on this line- -

- -Cut on this line- -

F-4. Since you don't want to run off and be left, find a man who enjoys a more leisurely pace; has time to live and love. Find one who likes to read, watch TV or the movies, fishing, good conversation, in short, one who wants to savor each moment of life and not just rush through it.

- -Cut on this line- -

F-5. You know that deep waters run slowly and, without doubt, you should find a man who feels the same way. Even emotions and love can't build up if you are always hurrying. There are millions of men who feel the same way as you. Look for one who enjoys the luxury of complete relaxation and lazing around.

- -Cut on this line- -

COMPATIBILITY–TWO

You will bring into your marriage not only your physical being, your talents and your mind, which may be called your physical inheritance, or Compatibility-One. But you also bring the whole accumulation of your experiences, what you have learned, attitudes acquired, likes and dislikes you have gathered along the way, and your unique way of looking at things. These may be called your social inheritance.

These, too, make compatibilities and incompatibilities. Although it is easier to adjust to them, or compensate for their lack, than it is to the Compatibility-One's, you should be aware of them and take them into consideration.

Years ago a woman brought to her husband a dowry, which was a sum of money, an estate, some property or an adequate gift. This is no longer the custom. But in reality every man and woman of today brings a dowry—their Compatibility-Two.

12

What Is Your Dowry?

Can two walk together, except they be agreed? The ancient Biblical personage Amos penned this question concerning human relationships twenty-five hundred years ago and it is still applicable when applied to the closest and most important of all relationships—marriage. The factor of Compatibility-Two seeks to approach this question posed by Amos and give guidelines to those wise couples who seek to provide the seeds for marital growth and development.

One might say that it is difficult to find two people working harmoniously together if they are not in agreement. The planet Earth has suffered two hot world wars and constant cold ones due to global disagreement, and marriages break up the same way. It is hard, if not impossible, to walk hand in hand as husband and wife, day in and day out, if one does not share the same attitudes, interests, cultural background, education, outlook on life. These are referred to as Compatibility-Two—your dowry.

Knowing the national death rates, an insurance company can know how many people of a particular age will die this year. This life expectancy is predicted by knowing such things as the age, sex, health, occupation, and so forth. They base their rates on these predictions. It has done well enough for them to become prosperous. What they cannot predict is which person will die. Statistics are valuable in this way. Similarly, colleges have used entrance examinations and high school grades to predict success in college. Their experience with this "predicting" has definitely shown that the best predictor of what a person will do in the future is what he has done in the past—"the most accurate predictor of future performance is past performance."

Studies of married couples over the last forty years have shown that certain psychosocial factors are important in predicting whether a couple can succeed in marriage or not; these have been called Compatibility-Two factors or "your dowry." Suppose, for instance, a couple has been dating. The young man has asked the woman to marry him. She has said, "Yes." They are now at their respective homes and doubts assail them. "Is this the right thing?" They know they are physically compatible, they took the Test. Being rational, they want some other assurances. There are marriage statistics and conclusions gleaned from hundreds of research projects. Here are nine of the most important variables:

1. *Premarital Pregnancy.* The studies are unanimous. The percentage of marriage failures is so high that it is usually better not to marry, even if the woman is pregnant. Contrary to popular thinking, it is the woman who holds it against the man.

2. *Length of Courtship and Engagement.* The longer the better. Another factor, if the courtship is scattered over with troubles and fusses, the chances are that the marriage will be also.

> "I just never was able to get serious about our marriage," said a young client, "because I knew down deep inside that I could never marry Albert. We just squabbled and fought all the time. One time I danced with another man and Albert became insanely jealous. I really could not respect him when comparing him with other men. I felt sorry for him when we broke up, that's all."

So, excessive quarreling during the engagement period is one of the most significant signs of trouble ahead, as in this case history.

> Jack wanted to have his way about things all the time. He had a terrible temper which disgusted me. To get what he wanted he became childish, threatening and angry. We did not quarrel while dating. It just seemed to start about three months after we were engaged.

3. *Age at Marriage and Differences in Age.* Up to your late twenties, the older you are, the better your chances of marital success. The average age at marriage for women is 20, for men it is 22. Any age younger than this could be considered a too early marriage. It seems that if the husband is much older or younger, i.e., six years or more than the woman, this will have a detrimental effect on the success probability.

> Joan and her fiance argued excessively about her friends in that he felt that she should stop seeing them. She could see no real reason to stop seeing men since she did not actually date them. On Joan's 18th birthday they broke up to the relief of both. The fiance, who was twenty-seven, felt that she was too young to know what it was all about, and did not take marriage seriously enough.

4. *Social Class and Residence.* The general trend in the studies indicate that the poorer you are *the lower the probability of success.* If you live in the country or small city your chances are better. Ghetto dwellers do indeed have shaky marital prospects.

5. *Previous Divorce and Divorced Parents.* If your intended spouse is a divorced man, the chances are 50–50 that he will be divorced again. However, the risk of failure is a little lower in the case of a divorced woman. Likewise children of divorced parents are more likely to be divorced. In general it can be said that *the happier the parents' marriage the happier will be the child's marriage.* Only one dissenting study was found.

A young client related: I have thought about it a lot and I feel that my problem comes from my parents' marriage. My dad used to come home drunk almost every night. When mother complained to him about spending the family's money, it inevitably started an argument. I can still remember her throwing a plate of spaghetti and meat balls at him and hitting me instead. All I can recall are those battles, tension, crying and alcohol. Even though I know that all marriages aren't like this and it depends on the specific people involved, I seem to see all marriages in terms of my parents' marriage. When I think seriously of marrying Betty I get all tense and upset. I have used every excuse imaginable for not sticking to a specific date. I just can't seem to shake the feeling that all marriages are doomed to failure. If this continues, I may not get married at all.

6. *Parental Conflict or Approval.* Individuals who report a great deal of conflict with their parents are high-risk mates. It is highly desirable to marry someone of whom your parents approve.

In the Western civilizations custom sanctions marriage arrangements without parental consent, though parents usually do manifest a sincere interest. Perhaps the old saying is true that "it takes two to get married, a willing daughter and an anxious mother." Parents with pronounced neurotic problems were most likely to arbitrarily interfere with their children's courtship and marriage. Mothers who themselves have unhappy marriages seem most anxious for their daughters to get married. A significant percent of elopements were by children of this type. The following clinical case presents several premarital factors including parental disapproval.

Laurie was an intelligent, charming daughter in an upper middle class family. At the university she had dated several of the leading men on campus and in her sophomore year became engaged to a highly desirable young man. At the beginning of the senior year he broke the engagement and announced that he was to marry the daughter of a wealthy, prominent family. Laurie, by chance, met an old home town acquaintance who was a high school dropout. Because he had lived "across the tracks," she had previously paid little attention to him. They became engaged, despite her parents' vigorous protests, and were married within a month. After the marriage she realized that her parents were indeed right, that she and her husband were misfits, both mentally and emotionally, that they had no mutual interests, and that he had no intention of completing high school. She returned home a wiser person and later secured a divorce.

7. *Education.* Most studies use nationwide samples and seem to indicate a significant relationship between years of education and marital success. What they are essentially saying is that the more formal education, that is, up through college, the better the chances of success. Indications are that if there is a difference in educational level, this difference will be less troublesome if the husband is the better educated. One further note should be added, there is often the tragic situation of the spouses growing apart when the husband continues his education and the wife doesn't. If at all possible, see to it that this does not happen to you. *Grow together or you will grow apart.*

8. *Religion.* Mixed faith marriages are extremely difficult: Protestant-Catholic, Christian-Jewish both show a higher incidence of divorce than do same-faith marriages. It has also been shown that persons who profess no particular religious beliefs maintain a divorce rate four times greater than religious persons. In marrying a professed atheist one is indeed making a poor gamble, even if both are atheists.

I think that I would have gone ahead and married Andy except he began objecting to my attending church on Sunday, the only day we had together. He said that he would just as soon have gone into the country and enjoyed God's natural beauty. I thoroughly enjoy attending church, and not because someone forced me to go. It is inspiring and helps me be a more cheerful person. We started to argue about it and he tried to make me stop going. I talked to my minister and decided that I wouldn't be happy living with a man who did not respect my religious need. I just don't really believe that any marriage can succeed where there is such a conflict.

9. *Mental Health.* All studies agree that good mental health is a predictor of satisfactory marital adjustment. It should be easily recognized that the first eight factors of Compatibility-Two are really based on emotional stability. Neurotic or psychotic conditions play a critical role in the death of many marriages, as well as an inability of a person to accept the possibility of marriage. Many men and women fear marriage. Why? It is quite normal to go through a period of doubt and tension during the period between the engagement and the day of the wedding. This is when one is saying good-bye to the single

life, with its many advantages and is preparing psychologically for this new, uncertain and perhaps threatening life. Society makes it easier for men to make this transition. Men joke about the "ball and chain" and "getting hooked." But the adjustment is as difficult, if not more so, for a woman.

Most individuals, do, of course, manage to overcome these feelings, but far too often these fears take on such gigantic forcefulness that they lead to irrational behavior. Studies typically isolate and discuss several such marriage fears.

1. *Loss of Romance.* As the marriage day approaches the woman is showered with all kinds of household objects to become entrenched in her many new responsibilities. She may hear people say, "She gave up her career to get married." This common attitude frightens many women because it subtly implies that life after the honeymoon is drudgery. To many, it is the *getting married that is beautiful, not being married.*

The husband, far too often, is not the romantic figure portrayed in novels and motion pictures, where the boyfriend or lover is idealized. As one young client put it, "Romeo and Juliet would not have stayed happy if they had married and lived a normal life." This attitude rubs off on many men and women. To illustrate the fact that this does occur after marriage perhaps may be unnecessary and self-evident but this is a typical case:

> "I never in my life would have thought that it could happen to us," said a twenty-nine year old client. "I can still vividly remember the many moonlit nights at the beach when I held her in my arms. I could feel her quiver at my touch. She seemed to want me so desperately; wanted to do anything and everything for me; nothing was too much trouble. She was the most exciting thing that had ever happened to me; no one had ever loved me that way before. That was five years ago, and the thing that most characterizes our marriage is the fact that the quiver is gone. About a month ago I went out and bought her some flowers. I sneaked up behind and kissed her on the back of the neck and told her that I loved her. Her only reply was 'I hope the fire is not too hot under the potatoes, I don't want supper to be ruined.' Actually it's not just that; but she is so critical of me now. She simply doesn't want me to touch her anymore. I don't know what to do—I want her back, so very much."

The impression received by psychologists in listening to case after case is that many persons conceive of marriage as being without romance and disappointing.

2. *Responsibility and Drudgery.* This fear is often behind the behavior of

individuals who are always getting engaged, but never marry. There are some understandably valid reasons for the man or woman who fears responsibility; sometimes he is too immature, or too young, and realizes it. Many women, because they want to be acceptable to friends, to parents or society, accept engagement rings, set a date, then panic.

An individual who has been indulged and the center of attention at home will be reticent to do anything for himself or anyone else. Fear of household drudgery may be caused from economic factors, but more often it comes from a woman's rejection of her role as a homemaker. A young client put it this way, "I won't be any man's slave," though she was willing to work overtime at the office. Women like this feel that the compensation for their work, independence, prestige, money, give them a place in the sun. They live the way they think a man lives. They are active rather than passive, competitive rather than comforting. Fear of responsibility can uncover a host of self-defeating mechanisms. The young man may secretly fear that he is not good enough for his fiancee. Surely, he feels, after marriage she will discover his inadequacies. Thus, unknown to himself, he subtly begins to drive her away, have doubts about her worth and wonder if he really does love her. Self-doubt, self-criticism, self-dislike will inevitably lead to self-defeat.

3. *Parental Attachment.* Related to fear of responsibility is a fear of leaving parents.

> This was the case with Marilea, who grew up in a strict home. When she received a visitor or a telephone call, her mother insisted on knowing every detail, and even when she was twenty-three her father waited up in the living room until her date said good night. When Marilea became engaged she was jubilant because she was not only "in love" but was also escaping.
>
> However, the marriage lasted only eight months. When she was divorced, she moved back in with her parents, instead of maintaining her small apartment which she could afford. Her parents continued to impose curfews and she continued to permit it.

The man or woman who seems to be fighting to be free of parents, yet is actually trying to hide a subconscious childish dependency, can pathetically hurt himself as well as the person who wants to marry him.

4. *Fear of Sex.* Fear of sex in our day is much more secretive because we like to think of ourselves as enlightened. As in the case of twenty-four year old Brenda, it can become quite open however.

> Brenda had been dating a desirable young man and was anxious to marry him. When he finally proposed, she was ecstatic.
>
> But two days before the ceremony she suddenly developed a severe case of hives which not only made her so uncomfortable that he could not touch her, but made her so unattractive that she insisted on postponing the wedding. Her family doctor suggested a trip to Florida which she took without her fiance. In two days the skin condition disappeared. She returned home, a new date set, and she again broke out in hives. Finally, through therapy with one of the authors, she realized that her skin eruptions had been her only way of saying what she had been afraid of saying aloud: "Don't touch me, I'm afraid of sex!"

Fears of sex often have their roots in childhood experiences. It is easy to see these fears when the individual has been reared in a home where sex had been kept in secrecy and considered vulgar or sinful. But even the apparently extroverted well-adjusted individual whose parents gave him adequate information can fall a victim. Various psychologists agree that even a very young child senses the difference between what the parent says and what the parent actually means. The mother who tries to cover up her embarrassment by answering questions with too vague or thorough an answer will only confuse the young child. Free discussion of sex and unrestrained exhibitionism are often self-conscious cover-ups for the parents' deeper feelings of shame and guilt. On the other hand, parents who give their child proper sex education, allow him to keep pets and watch the pets give birth, and then act cold, unloving and restrained toward each other create problems for their children which are just as injurious.

5. All too often the psychologist must counsel with a woman who is afraid of childbirth, as the following case illustrates.

> A nineteen-year-old woman, engaged to a "wonderful man," began having fainting spells whenever she was with her fiance. It was discovered that some years before a baby brother of the woman had died of meningitis. She had been jealous of him, and when he died she secretly blamed herself, imagining it had happened because she had wanted to be rid of him. She subconsciously feared ever having a baby, fearing her own guilt would let it die.

Sometimes a woman may fear sex and motherhood because she is afraid of growing up, in that motherhood puts her into another generation. Whatever may be the cause, if an individual is in love but afraid to marry, the cause is usually buried in the "unconscious." Even if vaguely aware, he has difficulty admitting to self and even more difficulty in admitting to the fiance, parents or friends. Hiding such fears will not make them disappear. The essential first step in solving them is to realize that he is not alone, not a freak—many people, both men and women, have suffered the same thing. With this knowledge, he will be able to admit his fears, an essential first step toward mental health and a happy marriage.

Is your dowry, your social inheritance, compatible with that of your mate? Take the following short test to find out. Put a check mark if your answer is "yes."

______ 1. Do you both have the approval of your parents?

______ 2. Are you both at least 20 but under 40 years old, and no more than six years apart in age?

______ 3. Has your mate never been married before?

______ 4. Have you dated or been engaged for at least one year?

______ 5. Does he or she come from a happy, well-adjusted home?

______ 6. Has your relationship been a close one, and relatively free from quarrels?

______ 7. Do you both practice moderation in personal habits (drinking, smoking)?

______ 8. Do you share the same ideas on the number of children desired and on how to raise or correct a child?

______ 9. Is he or she free of neurotic behavior, temper, and jealousy?

______ 10. Do you share similar religious beliefs or attend the same denominational church?

______ 11. Do you share the same attitudes about money and how it should be spent?

______ 12. Are neither of you overly afraid of or morbidly concerned with sex?

______ 13. Is he or she highly thought of by others as being dependable and reliable?

______ 14. Do you both have good educations?

______ 15. Does he or she like the job or profession in which he or she is employed?

Add up the number of check marks you have made. If the number is twelve or more, your marriage will have a much better chance of success. Obviously, you will want to compare answers and discuss your similarities and differences.

COMPATIBILITY—TWO CHECKLIST

This is a checklist intended to stimulate you to begin giving serious consideration to a few selected factors of your social inheritance. There are no right or wrong answers. The best answer is your frank, honest opinion. Because of this, no "correct" answers are given as is done on Compatibility-One. You will, however, need to carefully compare your answers with those expressed by your spouse or future spouse. Compare, and if too many differences seem to exist read or re-read this chapter. By combining the self-knowledge gleaned from this checklist with that from the marriage compatibility test, you may be able to dramatically improve your mate selection ability.

We all have needs, interests, attitudes, and tolerances; some are more important than others. What are yours? Imagine that you have met a very attractive person with whom you would like to seriously associate and perhaps marry. How important would each of these factors be to you? Answer thoughtfully and truthfully. Check only one in each group.

EDUCATION—I would require of a spouse

A. a person with graduate work or professional training. ———

B. a college degree. ———

C. some college work. ———

D. high school graduation. ———

E. it really does not matter. ———

RELIGION—

A. is the most important thing in life; I live it daily. ———

B. is very important; attend or work in church regularly. ———

C. I attend church occasionally. ———

D. Not a churchgoer; I have my own belief. ———

E. I have little or no interest in religion. ———

My religion is—

A. Catholic ______
B. Protestant ______
C. Jewish ______
D. Other____________ ______
E. None in particular ______

I would marry a person of the following religion—

A. Catholic ______
B. Protestant ______
C. Jewish ______
D. Other____________ ______
E. None in particular ______

DIVORCE—

A. I do not object to marrying someone who has been married once before. ______
B. I do not object to marrying someone who has been married at least twice before. ______
C. I would not marry a divorced person. ______

CHILDREN—I would

A. marry a person without children. ______
B. marry if previous children are not living at home. ______
C. say children do not bother me. ______
D. prefer someone with children. ______
E. prefer a person who does not want any children. ______

SEX—Has been or will be

A. a necessary part of my life. ______
B. something to enjoy very much. ______
C. something I can take or leave. ______
D. something I can do without. ______

My work is—

A. blue collar ______
B. white collar ______

C. technical ______
D. professional ______
E. my own business ______

I would like my spouse to be—

A. blue collar ______
B. white collar ______
C. technical ______
D. professional ______
E. no preference ______

My income range is—

A. $8,000 or below ______
B. $8,000 to $15,000 ______
C. $15,000 or above ______

My spouse's income should range—

A. $8,000 or below ______
B. $8,000 to $15,000 ______
C. $15,000 or above ______
D. I do not want my spouse to work. ______

Drinking—I would

A. not marry anyone who drinks at all. ______
B. object only to drinking and then driving a car. ______
C. not object to social drinking. ______
D. join in a social drink. ______
E. not object to anyone not an alcoholic. ______

Indicate your interest in each of the following activities by writing the numbers 1, 2 or 3. Use the following code:

(1) very interested
(2) indifferent
(3) not interested

1. Dancing, ballroom ______
2. Dancing, modern ______

3. Dancing, country ______
4. Dancing, all type ______
5. Parties, formal ______
6. Parties, informal ______
7. Parties, outdoor ______
8. Parties, all type ______
9. Spectator sports ______
10. Swimming and water sports ______
11. Bowling ______
12. Golf ______
13. Camping and hiking ______
14. All outdoor sports ______
15. Reading, magazines and newspapers ______
16. Reading, fiction ______
17. Reading, biography and historical ______
18. Reading, business or technical ______
19. Reading, all types ______
20. Playing bridge ______
21. Playing poker ______
22. Playing chess ______
23. Playing all competitive games ______
24. Music, folk ______
25. Music, classical ______
26. Music, popular ______
27. Music, country ______
28. Music, all music ______
29. Stage shows or plays ______
30. Concerts and ballet ______
31. Movies ______
32. Television ______
33. All visual arts ______
34. Social clubs ______
35. Political meetings ______
36. Church work and socials ______

37. All social and club work ______
38. Bland foods ______
39. Fancy foods ______
40. Spicy foods ______
41. Plain home cooking ______
42. Photography ______
43. Gardening ______
44. Crafts (sewing, woodwork, etc.) ______
45. Varied hobbies ______

Go back over the above list and choose three that you enjoy doing MOST. Place the corresponding numbers on the three lines opposite.

______
______
______

COMPATIBILITY–THREE

After marriage there is a cooling-off period lasting from some six months to possibly a year and a half. If, during this time, the couple is able to build a deep love to replace the fiery and exciting love of before marriage, they have an excellent chance of building something permanent. If this is not done, as happens in so many marriages, nothing but the icy coals are left; and these often turn to hostility and hatred. Therefore, it is true that love must be nurtured or it will die.

13

Nurturing Love

Connubial happiness is a thing of too fine a texture to be handled roughly. It is a tender plant, which will not bear even the touch of unkindness; a delicate flower, which indifference will chill and suspicion blast. It must be watered by the showers of tender affection, expanded by the cheering glow of kindness, and guarded by the impregnable barrier of unshaken confidence. Thus matured, it will bloom with fragrance in every season of life, and sweeten even the loneliest of declining years.

Thomas Sprat

Just as important to marital happiness and success is what we have called Compatibility–Three—the factor of growth and development as the marriage matures. Most couples expect both permanence and happiness in marriage. The question of just how happy must a marriage be is not easily answered because happiness is such a complex, subjective mental state. Often, in the clinic, while studying case after case, the marriage counsellor sadly realizes that perhaps Thoreau was correct. Perhaps most couples do indeed "live lives of quiet desperation." For we find that lasting happiness and satisfaction in marriage seem to be most difficult to find. More often there is a quiet, puzzled sense of something lacking, something beyond one's comprehension to recognize, or to remedy.

Movies, TV, *True Confession* stories and some books have built false expectations of married rapture, of every day "living on the mountain tops," into the thinking of some young people. Life is not just that way. Just as we could not live happily in an environment of continual sunshine, so a couple cannot be satisfied, nor will they find everyday life and love the way it was when they sat entwined just before saying "good night" at the end of a pleasant date. Nor will they find it filled with the passionate and emotional anticipation they experienced when they discussed their impending marriage. These are highlights of love. Everyday is different.

After marriage, when they wake up in the morning and he needs a shave and to get rid of his half sleepy and half burly attitude, it is different from the nights before marriage when he came to visit her with face clean, all dressed in his best, wide awake and pleasant. She, too, will look different with hair in curlers, no make-up and irritable because she wanted another hour of "beauty sleep" (and he may agree she needs it). This is not just like the books described it nor like the movies portrayed the awakening of the movie queen and her hero. But, after getting over the shock of seeing life in reality, they can build a marriage relationship where their beings so fuse that things are no longer "mine" or "yours" but "ours." But even then they do maintain a bit of "separateness"; few husbands are so "one" that they use the same toothbrush.

Adolescent love—the good night kiss, repeated a dozen times—is a necessary phase of romantic development. It is passion, infatuation, dotingness, enamorment, fascination, all rolled into one, and is a preamble to real love. There are many who believe that "true love" is not present in brides and bridegrooms, only in those who have lived together through good days and bad, through joys and sorrows—indeed, for years. Love for the husband and wife implies the inability to conceive of life without each other. This means a mutual interdependence on each other. True happiness also becomes a reality, years after the marriage ceremony, when this realization is achieved. Love is *giving, not getting.* Love is going to work every day, working hard so that money can be earned which will give to the beloved the necessities and a few luxuries of life. Love is not kisses and "sweet words," it is doing for the other.

Psychology has consistently shown that the problem of marriage is one of an unending struggle between two more or less imperfect human beings trying to find a mental, emotional and spiritual equilibrium which will bring them happiness and a feeling of completeness. Sooner or later the young couple realizes that the marriage ceremony is not complete fulfillment but only the beginning of love. The bliss that it can bring is not something given at the start, but is achieved at the end. Marriage in essence is a challenge, an adventure, an experiment. It is not realized all at once, but lived from day to day, drawing heavily from personality strengths of forgiveness, courage, patience and love, for its ultimate fulfillment.

A deeply hurt bitter client recently remarked that, "No one these days thinks he or she is going to be happy in marriage. That's the main problem."

She must be disagreed with. Few if any couples embark on marriage with anything but happiness in mind. They do not, unfortunately, think of it as the fragile, tender plant that it is, which must be thought about and worked for, protected, and carefully nourished. It is imperative that the individual accept for himself the determination that nothing shall damage or destroy this thing that my spouse and I have created. No third party shall tamper with it, no happening shall be allowed to undermine it. This that we have created is beautiful and living and we will keep it safe no matter what happens.

With this in mind the couple will not allow contempt to grow into a giant, will not hold grudges against each other or suffer in silence. And it is true—familiarity can breed contempt. Remember, politeness both in private and public is always desirable.

Little things, such as knocking on the bedroom door before entering, or never opening personal letters without permission, although you both may feel that it wouldn't matter, should not be overlooked. One should have no, or at least very few, secrets from each other. Explain even the little embarrassing occurrences which sometimes cause big misunderstandings. You may well not like some of her friends or she yours but never quarrel over them or inflict the undesirables upon each other unnecessarily.

> "Our trouble," began Jane, "is that very seldom can we ever have time to ourselves. My husband is a minister and never has time for me or the children. He is gone all the time to visit church members or attend meetings or a thousand and one other things. Doctor, do you know I was counting the other day and it has been two months since he has touched me affectionately. In the last two years I've had to almost beg him to make love to me. He's always so tired or has other people's problems on his mind. I don't like it. It makes me feel like a woman of the streets, having to beg my husband." By this time Jane was crying uncontrollably. "Sometimes when I'm lying beside him in the dark I feel so empty, frustrated, so alone and unwanted. Then I want to just cry out, "God forgive me if I've sinned, but why doesn't he love me?' Doctor, why is it that I'm so jealous of any woman my husband talks to? Even when he pays attention to the little old ladies in the sewing circle I get hurt, so resentful." She concluded by stating several times in different ways "if only he had time for me, oh God, if only he would just do nothing more than pat me on the back in a caring manner it would mean so much."

Any friendship, any vocation, in fact, any situation no matter how worthy, simply is not important enough to interfere with your marriage. When you get on each other's nerves talk it through at the first opportunity and be ready and willing to compromise.

The healing balm for most difficulties of living together is the shifting of attention from oneself to the husband or wife. Only in this manner can you securely build up an edifice of understanding and tolerance to pervade daily life together and keep your marriage vows in good condition.

Compromise is something which must be constantly kept in mind. One spouse is bound to dominate in certain areas. Typically, the wife determines social and domestic decisions, and the man the car and finances. But often couples fail to realize or accept that these areas overlap each other and thus each should have a voice in all decisions. The childishness of most matrimonial quarrels is painfully obvious. Talking things out without sulking or displaying injured feelings or harboring grudges is a primary lesson which must be learned by partners in matrimony.

In the first years of married life the companionship of doing everything together is glorious, and some couples think that the thrill of it will last a lifetime. They seem to take it for granted that marriage means the end of both physical and mental privacy. They don't realize that to most people a certain amount of aloneness is a very necessary aspect of a good life. In the overcrowded conditions of urban living this need becomes an acute one. But even where there is plenty of room, the traditional attitude of the marriage partners and the time-worn restrictions placed upon them by friends and relatives often bring about the same end result. This is not to advocate separate facilities or amusement for the family, but merely an attitude of respect toward individuality of thought and action.

> Bob was an avid fisherman. Every weekend found him on some lake or stream. Sometimes he left Friday afternoon after work and at others on Saturday morning. His wife considered herself a "fishing widow."
>
> She had tried going with him a couple of times, but this was worse. He rented a cabin for her and their two boys. Then she had to take care of the children, cook and clean the fish. Bob stayed out in the boat or along the bank. She didn't get to see any more of him than when she stayed home, for Bob fished both day and night.
>
> This was the cause of their break-up. In her divorce petition, she alleged that he was rude and selfish and not a good husband nor father because of his fishing.

Conscious sacrifice, the kind one talks and thinks about, breeds self-pity and is artificial. This kind of sacrifice should have no place in the relationship of marriage, any more than it should exist in any other type of partnership. The intelligent attitude is that marriage is a partnership and that each partner must make a success of it. Obviously, the object of any partnership is to succeed. Nothing in the world is worth having if it is not worth working for, and no success is achieved without considerable effort.

The capacity to love is a talent, which must be developed through training. If one has a talent for music, can he expect to keep that gift if he never uses his voice or his fingers, if he never practices? Love is the same, you must use it to keep it in working condition. Many divorces come about because it seldom enters the couples' minds to practice love. But even a love filled marriage will not last unless a great deal of effort, intelligence, understanding and an even greater amount of effort are put into the desire to make the partnership work.

The question of money in marriage can be a difficult one. Single people, spending their own money, with no one else to answer to seem to function nicely. When they marry, instantly, financial trouble can and will grow like weeds. It's not always the lack of money that causes this thorny growth, but the disposition of family funds. The answer is a businesslike cooperation and acceptance of a family budget that, while it need not be adhered to relentlessly, for that takes most of the joy out of life, will nevertheless keep one out of serious trouble.

One suggestion that may work for you is a joint bank account into which all revenue goes. Early in the month make a list of bills on a large manila envelope, the bills themselves being kept inside. This and the check book are always available to either partner to consult and study. Around the end of the first week of each month, perhaps on Sunday evening, these records are brought out and discussed. At that time all financial problems and resentments or misunderstandings are talked over. At this time perhaps you can make monthly plans, decide how often you can eat out, arrange for future insurance premiums, car payments, bills, literally clear up the financial horizon as far as possible. This, or a similar system, will eliminate much of the friction that ruins marriages. If you talk the whole thing out twelve times a year, you will find a lessening need to discuss the subject between times.

"Mark takes all the family earnings and spends them on himself," said a college freshman to her counsellor. "He buys all kinds of things for himself and his car. I plead with him to let me have a little for bills and our baby. He just doesn't seem to care. All he ever says to me is that it is his money and he'll decide how to spend it."

But Mark related to the counsellor a different story. "I'll bet my wife didn't tell you that two years ago she told me she was pregnant. I loved her so we got married. It turned out that she hadn't been pregnant at all. Before we were married she was proud of my car. Now she wants to spend my pay check her way. I work hard for the money I make and I want to have some fun with it. But no, we have to live in an apartment we can't afford because she doesn't want to live in an average neighborhood. Besides, the real problem is that she doesn't know how to spend money.

She bought a $75 dress and $35 pair of shoes only last week. I really don't care anymore if we get a divorce. At least I'll be able to have fun again."

The extravagant husband and the practical wife must maintain some working agreement or nagging will result. It is just as difficult when the situation is reversed and the wife is extravagant.

A large number of differences that are labelled "mental cruelty" start from small, insignificant situations that are unnecessarily allowed a foothold. Irritability brought on by any number of conditions may breed numerous situations which could wreck the marriage. This is where complete candor between spouses is imperative. The feeling of complete freedom of speech is absolutely necessary. A headache or indigestion may cause an avalanche of bitterness. A discussion started while hungry or tired or during that period in the month when the wife is not feeling her best may bring on a real quarrel. Two persons living intimately together must take all things into account. Situations of dislike, contempt and pettiness grow from simple misunderstandings that usually can be easily avoided. Human behavior cannot change overnight, and marriage must not be considered a reform school. This is a well established truth that we have all heard and believe, yet we go right on irrationally expecting miracles to happen.

A sense of humor is a wondrous gift that can help out in temperamental difficulties. By a sense of humor, psychologists don't mean the teasing or wisecracking that many adults carry over from childhood. A happy home must be delivered of the husband who turns every serious conversation into a farce by a wisecrack. And the wisecracking wife is just as bad.

The important rule of not allowing a third party to interfere is one the couple must thoroughly agree upon even before marriage. You may have to remind yourselves of it occasionally because friends sometimes make bad situations where they really don't exist. And families continue to interfere and young people keep on letting them. Children should be included on the list of nuisances, because so often couples come to blows over such things as discipline and education. Psychologists have found that children get along better when considered happy additions to the marriage rather than rulers of the home. Parents should discuss the children and their problems when they are in bed, not when the children are listening. Whichever parent starts the discipline should finish it without criticism or interference from the other. Children often play one parent against the other, if it can be done, and many marriages show weaknesses of this sort.

Such little things as these are really the big things in this relationship we call marriage and not caring enough to listen is probably one of the most inconsiderate blunders of all. This is because it creates, more devastatingly than most anything else, an atmosphere in the home of not caring and not loving.

> Recently, a client whose husband went into a television trance every night made an unsuccessful attempt to gain his attention by announcing in a matter of fact way that she had taken a lover, had withdrawn all their savings and was leaving him. To this she received not even a grunt of reply. She then grabbed him by the throat and shouted, "Weren't you listening to what I said? Listen to me, damn you." The husband, without taking his eyes off the football game, kindly responded by patting her hand and saying, "Yes, of course, I love you, dear." It is not too difficult to see that she probably did not believe him. Who can blame her?

The implication here is not that loving words lack the power to convey love, but that words alone cannot do the job. A husband communicates to his wife that she is loved by listening, for one thing, and all the sonorous phrases in the language won't make up for not hearing what is said.

This matter of communication between husbands and wives is an important factor in marriage. It means not only hearing what is said, but knowing the other person so well as to understand what is meant even when it is not so well expressed.

> "Women! I'll never understand them," muttered Jim as Meg stalked out of the room. "What have I done this time?" he called after her.
>
> "If you don't know, I'm not going to tell you," sobbed Meg.
>
> "Blasted women."

Jim was confused; Meg was brokenhearted. Are women that hard to understand? Even they will answer with a resounding "Yes!" And for good reason. But there is some hope that they can be understood. The difficulty lies in the roles society has given them and the early training they receive for these roles. The vast majority of all females, from toddler to grandmother, still desire above all else to be married and have a family.

Boys are taught to be strong, forceful, dynamic and logical, that is, masculine. They are urged to prepare for a career. The boy is taught very little, if anything, about girls. If he asks a question about sister or some other girl, he is told, "She is a girl. Girls are different." No one explains how or why she is different, and he grows up in ignorance.

The little girl, on the other hand, is taught from infancy about boys. She learns how to flirt on her daddy's knee. How to catch a man is her prime subject. If she has good examples to pattern after and practice on, she will learn her lesson well.

Women can be divided into two main categories: Career Girls and Housewives. There are other groups, but these will do for our purpose. Man understands easiest the Career Girl. She works with men and has learned to communicate with them. She "thinks like a man." When a man marries one of these, the two can communicate and all is well, for a while. The trouble begins when she becomes a mother. At this time she begins the transition into a housewife. This happens whether she gives up her work or not. If a Career Girl stops working, she becomes a Housewife in six months to a year. Then the trouble in understanding begins.

For Carol, the transition was quick. She became pregnant a month after marriage. Her feelings were mixed. Sure, she intended to have a family "someday," but not so soon. Her husband was happy, so she looked forward with him to the arrival.

The first few months were wonderful. Their lives were changed very little except the husband was more attentive to her. They were close and in love and wanted to make a home for the baby. But six months later, things changed.

"I'm so big and clumsy looking," thought Carol. "Ralph can't love me now. I look like a pig," she sobbed into her pillow.

Ralph soon found that he was constantly having to reassure her. "You have never been more beautiful to me," he would say. "That's my son kicking around in there and you make a beautiful pair."

Ralph's friends and father had told him that Carol would act this way. They didn't tell him why, except that "she is a woman."

Carol had been taught all her life that physical appearance was of supreme importance in getting and keeping a husband. Now she was fat, and men don't like fat women. She didn't differentiate pregnancy fat from "eating-too-much fat," as her husband had. She was insecure. Questions buzzed around in her head. Will she be a good mother? Will the baby be healthy and whole? Can she take the pain of childbirth? This was all new to her and she was inexperienced. This is the unknown to her—frightening—she's scared. When you are scared, you lose confidence.

Ralph had been taught to welcome new experiences—a challenge—a chance to prove yourself. He thus welcomed marriage and now fatherhood.

Carol had been taught that when a new situation arises, a man (father, brother, sweetheart or husband) will take care of it. But they couldn't take care of this for her.

She lived over it. Most women do. And, as a result, she became more self-confident and mature—but less understandable.

A new father learns a shocking fact. He is now relegated to second position. The baby comes first. If baby is hungry, he must be fed; if wet, must be changed. This is true regardless of whether father feels loving toward his wife. And babies have an uncanny instinct about when is the most inconvenient time to cry. The wife *ceases to be a wife,* so the husband thinks, *and becomes a mother.* If the wife returns to work, their social life is not affected too much. If she does not go back to work, she soon becomes a housewife.

With each additional child, she is pushed more toward becoming a housewife. The real crisis begins to build when children start to school. Then she has twelve terrible years ahead. During this time she is continually under conflicting pressures. Who comes first? Husband, children, herself? Usually the children win out. The husband is, after all, an adult and can take care of himself. He is gradually relegated to third place and feels left out.

Mothers are prone to deny themselves to give to the children, and children are tyrants. The mother feels "used" and the father feels "pushed out" by his own children.

> One evening Cliff came from work very excited. "John is being transferred to Chicago next month and offered to sell us his cabin on the lake for what he paid for it. What do you say?"
>
> The excited children cried out, "Can we spend weekends there, Dad?" "I can try out my new rod and reel!" "Oh, boy! Swimming all summer."
>
> "Now wait, children. It's up to your mother. We would have to use the money we have been saving for the new carpeting and living room suite. What do you say, honey? I know you have been really economizing in order to save that money; and I know how important it is to you; but we would save money on vacations and the kids would enjoy it. We'll never be able to get that kind of a bargain again."
>
> Rita smiled as the kids jumped around her. "Of course, we'll buy it, dear. The living room can wait a while longer."

No one suspected that beneath that smile she was crying deep inside. She knew what was in store for her. The frantic weekend packing, the cooking and keeping house in two houses instead of one. The extra expense of guests who "just dropped by." The new boat and ski rigs she knew would soon become a necessity. No more relaxing vacations in motels where she didn't have to cook or clean. She was also busy figuring on how she could make slip covers to hide the patch on the arm of the sofa, if they didn't spend too much at the lake this summer.

Fortunately for Rita, Cliff was a very perceptive husband. He came into the kitchen and put his arm around her.

"I called John and told him we would take the cabin. I know this will make life rough for you, honey. We'll have fun while you do the work. What say I call Bob and Becky and offer them the cabin one weekend a month if they take our kids? They enjoy the kids and like having them around since they don't have any of their own. Then you and I can spend a nice quiet weekend alone, go out to eat and see a show. Would you like that?"

Rita threw her arms around his neck and kissed him soundly. "I love you," she cried.

But to come back to Jim and Meg and her sobbing reply, "If you don't know, I'm not going to tell you." This is a common expression by women. It always mystifies men. They don't understand it. Well, let a woman explain it to you.

"When a woman uses the statement, 'If you don't know, I'm not going to tell you,' it is an effort to save herself from humiliation even greater than she feels has already been heaped upon her. By using this phrase, she is hoping that her husband, on his own, will notice that she is wearing a new dress, has changed her hairstyle or color, has changed the furniture, or something else that she was sure would be quite obvious to him. When he did not notice these things immediately, she interprets it that he does not pay very much attention to her or how she performs her wifely functions.

"This is a great blow to her self-respect for her self-respect is in direct proportion to the respect shown her by her family and friends. It more especially mirrors her husband's respect for her.

"Women who use the phrase, 'If you don't know . . .' will also be likely to use another phrase that is mystifying to men. *You don't love me, just my body.* This statement is *never* spoken by a woman who feels appreciated by her husband. All women realize that sex (her body) is very important in the image her husband has of her, and she of him. But no wife wants to be made to feel as though she is regarded in the same way as is a prostitute. This is exactly how her husband makes her feel when he says, or implies, that it is her *duty* to relieve his sexual tensions whether she wants to or not. This is especially true when he does not sufficiently try to arouse her interest in sex.

When I speak of arousing her interest in sex, I do not mean kissing, fondling and caressing her just immediately prior to actual intercourse. No amount of kissing and petting at that time will put a woman in the mood for sex if during the previous several hours the husband has done nothing but complain. Quite the contrary. It will be irritating. If she is willing to submit at all, it will be just that—submission, and, *for God's sake, hurry up and get it over with.* Of course, a husband does not have to complain all the time in order to put his wife in such a negative mood. The simple act of ignoring her will suffice.

Another problem for the housewife is boredom. This is a fact of life for her and often a principal cause of divorce. Even though she is constantly busy, it is work that holds no intellectual challenge. She tries to relieve this boredom in various ways. Moving furniture is usually a sign of boredom. She is trying to bring some variety into her life. Most of the things in her life cannot be changed. The arrangement of the furniture, the color of the walls and slip covers can. These changes may indicate more than boredom; she may be giving outlet to her creativity as well.

How about shoes, hats, jewelry? Does she seem to have more than you think she needs? Boredom is a factor here as well. But she may also be trying to bolster her ego. Trying to feel, as well as look, attractive. When friends see her large wardrobe they feel that she has a good husband who cares about her. The fact that she may have bought them herself and even had to fight her husband to get them does not diminish their importance. She is buying prestige, not only for herself but for her husband as well. *If she has to buy a feeling of prestige, her husband must not be giving it to her.* If she says, "I haven't a thing to wear," when her closet is crowded with clothes, what she really means is that all her friends have seen her in all of them and she will feel a loss of prestige if she has to wear them again.

Our career girl turned housewife also gave us some insight into why women become "joiners." "Women are usually very social creatures. A woman will join a group, not for what it stands for but for the *adult* social contact. She may not really care much about pollution but will become active in a group dealing with it simply because someone she admires does. These groups are usually short lived as the individual women become bored with it.

"To add excitement (and glamour) to her life, she will sometimes take a job. In most cases she soon finds paid work is just as boring as being a housewife. After the first excitement of being 'out in the world' has worn off, she is just as bored, and much more tired than before. The fact that most men are in jobs that are just as boring has not entered her mind. She feels that women are discriminated against and that men are responsible for all her problems—enter Women's Lib."

This housewife's remarks point up, again, the importance of communication between husband and wife. Many of the problems she discussed were directly attributable to the "she/he thinks that he/she thinks" syndrome. Any time you speak, there are at least three meanings to your words: what you said, what you meant and what the other person thought you meant. The three should be the same, but in an intensely intimate and personal relationship, as between husband and wife, they almost never are.

> Dick and Betty went to friends for dinner. On the way home, Dick said: "That certainly was a delicious roast Lauri had for dinner."

Just a simple statement, meaning he had enjoyed the dinner—at least, that was all he intended. But how did Betty understand it? If she feels secure in her own ability to cook and in her relationship with Dick, she will probably accept it as just that and agree. However, if Dick had complained about her "poor cooking—"When will you ever learn to fry an egg?"—or if he had ignored her at the dinner and talked more to Lauri, she will understand it quite differently.

> "He doesn't like my cooking. He doesn't even want to be with me. He wishes he had married Lauri, or that Isabella Jones he used to go with. He doesn't love me." She thinks all of these things and out loud she storms: "You don't love me anymore. Why didn't you marry that damned Isabella?"
>
> Poor Dick is completely dumbfounded and cannot understand how such a nice evening has been suddenly spoiled.

What is meant by Compatibility-Three? It is the developing compatibility, for a couple either grows more compatible as they live together or they become less compatible and grow apart. It depends on whether they can understand each other better. There are those who marry in the first flush of infatuation and never nurture their feelings enough to allow them to become love. In this day of super-sex it is easy to mistake sexual attraction for love. There is a difference.

Sexual desire can be caused by loneliness, the need to belong, by vanity, wish to conquer, to hurt or even destroy, just as easily as it can be stimulated by love. It obviously can blend with or be stimulated by *any strong emotion,* of which love is only one. One may even have such a strong need for love that its physical expression becomes a compulsion.

> Such was the case with a beautiful young client seen by one of the authors. Her presenting problem was an intense, demanding need to be loved. At the time she was first seen, she was sleeping with from three to four different men every week but never experiencing the deep fulfilling relationship she so desperately desired. With deep throated cries of

desperation she questioned hardly above a whisper, "Doctor, why can't I control myself? How long is it going to take? Why can't I love? Everyone has told me how beautiful I am. Why can't they tell me that I am good?" And in tearful agony exclaimed, "I want to be good. God help me to be good." We wish it were possible to report that she had improved, but when last seen, she was living under similar circumstances and was still a miserably unhappy human being.

The psychological nature of "falling in love" is frequently a mistaken phenomenon of life. It is rather improbable that couples who "fall in love at first sight," in the usual sense of the word, attain a mature love life over night. The majority of people seem to feel that they must "fall in love" before they can be happy in marriage. Nothing could be further from the truth. However, it is imperative that mutual attraction exist from the very beginning. The body chemistry of attraction must be there at the beginning or it is likely to be artificial and will seldom, if ever, develop later on. But just as critical is the need for each partner to have a good sex education. This means a capacity to learn to make adjustments and the realization that perfect sexual compatibility does not exist, but that good sexual relations do.

For, as this book has repeatedly explained, lasting love is the result of years of concerted effort, of mutual enjoyment and mutual suffering. Love is the reward of a successfully lived marriage, not the foundation of a honeymoon. Thus, we have emphasized throughout that most marriages would turn out more satisfactorily if the contracting parties gave less thought to love and more to mental and emotional compatibilities, and every-day matters such as financial budgets, child rearing practices, social cooperation and willingness to share responsibility. Throughout we have contended that marriages would be happier if we planned them on the deeper consideration of occupational, social and intellectual compatibilities, responsibilities toward childen and state, and mutual helpfulness.

To enumerate the important factors of a happy marriage is difficult. And it is important to remember that perfect marriages like perfect human beings, simply don't exist. However, good people and good marriages can and do exist and result from giving serious attention to such considerations as we have discussed and the need for both partners to possess a mature sense of self-esteem and identity. Each is able to recognize and accept each other's values, beliefs, assets, liabilities, and feelings. There is a strong sense of joint and individual responsibility, plus the feeling that marriage has not deprived them of a career, enjoyment or freedom. Happily married couples feel that the formation of a well integrated family is primary to their well-being and that every day family tasks are to be undertaken without feelings of self-sacrifice or martyrdom. Likewise, they are able to laugh at themselves and each other and are able to express anger instead of harboring it or holding a grudge. They will listen to each other and be willing to forgive and forget.

Love is a creative and artistic undertaking, as much as is living itself. Rather than teach our young people any other idea than this, let us institute objective training in the art of love, and teach that they must be responsible for their erotic passions, just as they are responsible for other tendencies in their behavior. A critical shortage of mature love exists. This chapter will end the way it began by stating that the deeper joy of love begins after the marriage ceremony when Compatibility-Three, through growth, is achieved.

Young love is a flame; very pretty, often hot and fierce, but still only light and flickering. The love of the older and disciplined heart is as coals, deep-burning, unquenchable.

H. W. Beecher

FACTOR A

1. yes	118. yes
2. no	119. yes
3. no	120. no
4. no	125. yes
17. yes	127. yes
25. no	130. no
26. yes	131. yes
31. no	138. yes
38. yes	143. no
40. no	151. no
44. no	152. no
46. yes	167. no
47. yes	171. no
48. no	176. no
68. no	178. yes
81. no	180. no
85. no	182. yes
88. yes	186. no
89. yes	187. yes
94. yes	188. no
95. yes	190. yes
97. yes	194. yes
101. yes	195. yes
108. no	196. no
111. no	201. no
114. yes	207. yes
116. yes	208. yes

number correct

FACTOR B

3. no	123. no
10. no	141. no
11. no	144. no
19. no	146. no
23. no	147. no
25. no	167. no
29. no	170. no
32. yes	172. no
39. no	177. no
41. no	180. no
47. no	181. no
65. no	182. no
70. no	191. no
71. no	193. no
72. no	194. no
74. no	196. no
76. no	198. no
79. no	201. no
81. no	202. no
96. yes	203. no
99. yes	204. no
114. no	205. no
115. no	206. no

number correct

FACTOR C

17. yes	94. yes
18. no	95. yes
21. yes	97. yes
25. no	99. yes
28. no	102. yes
37. yes	103. yes
40. no	114. no
41. no	115. no
47. no	119. yes
48. no	147. no
50. yes	168. yes
70. no	169. yes
71. no	171. yes
72. no	184. yes
76. no	185. no
82. yes	189. yes
85. yes	192. no
88. yes	199. no
90. yes	204. no

number correct

FACTOR D

153. 2	51. 3
154. 2	52. 1
155. 3	53. 3
156. 2	54. 3
157. 3	55. 2
158. 2	56. 1
159. 3	57. 1
160. 3	58. 1
161. 2	59. 2
162. 3	60. 3
163. 1	61. 1
164. 2	62. 2
165. 3	63. 2
166. 2	

number correct

FACTOR E

4. yes	113. yes
14. yes	122. yes
15. yes	126. no
21. yes	127. no
24. yes	136. yes
34. no	137. yes
35. yes	139. yes
64. yes	140. yes
66. yes	142. no
69. yes	145. no
70. yes	148. yes
73. no	149. yes
75. yes	150. yes
78. no	173. yes
80. yes	174. yes
83. no	175. yes
84. no	179. yes
91. no	181. yes
92. yes	185. yes
93. yes	188. no
98. yes	192. yes
100. yes	197. yes
104. no	199. yes
110. no	200. yes
112. yes	207. yes

number correct

FACTOR F

3. no	45. no
5. yes	48. no
6. yes	49. yes
7. yes	67. yes
8. yes	77. yes
9. yes	86. yes
10. yes	87. yes
11. yes	96. yes
12. yes	105. yes
13. yes	106. no
16. yes	107. yes
18. yes	109. yes
22. no	117. yes
27. no	121. yes
30. yes	124. yes
32. no	128. no
33. no	133. yes
36. yes	134. yes
40. no	135. yes
42. yes	141. no
43. yes	208. yes

number correct

MALE CODE CONVERSION CHART

	A	B	C	D	E	F
1	38 or more	34 or more	26 or more	25 or more	37 or more	26 or more
2	34–37	30–33	21–25	21–24	33–36	22–25
3	30–33	26–29	17–20	14–20	28–32	16–21
4	26–29	22–25	12–16	11–13	24–27	11–15
5	25 or less	21 or less	11 or less	10 or less	23 or less	10 or less

FEMALE CODE CONVERSION CHART

	A	B	C	D	E	F
1	40 or more	37 or more	24 or more	25 or more	43 or more	25 or more
2	37–39	33–36	19–23	21–24	38–42	21–24
3	32–36	28–32	14–18	14–20	33–37	15–20
4	28–31	24–27	10–13	13–11	28–32	14–11
5	27 or less	23 or less	9 or less	10 or less	27 or less	10 or less

MATCHING CHART

	M	F	M	F	M	F	M	F	M	F
A	1	1 & 2	2	1 & 2 & 3	3	3 & 4	4	4 & 5	5	4 & 5
B	1	1 & 2 & 3	2	1 & 2 & 3	3	3 & 4	4	3 & 4 & 5	5	4 & 5
C	1	1 & 2 & 3	2	2 & 3	3	3 & 4	4	4 & 5	5	4 & 5
D	1	1 & 2 & 3	2	1 & 2 & 3	3	3 & 4	4	4 & 5	5	5
E	1	1 & 2	2	2 & 3	3	3 & 4	4	3 & 4 & 5	5	4 & 5
F	1	1 & 2	2	1 & 2 & 3	3	3 & 4	4	3 & 4 & 5	5	4 & 5

FOR FURTHER READING

ARKOFF, A. *Adjustment and Mental Health.* New York: McGraw-Hill, 1968.

BARDWICK, J. *Psychology for Women.* New York: Harper and Row, 1971.

BERGLER, E. *Counterfeit Sex.* New York: Grune and Stratton, 1958.

BLOOD, R. *Marriage.* Second Edition. New York: Free Press, 1969.

CATTELL, R. *The Scientific Analysis of Personality.* Baltimore: Penguin Books, 1965.

ERIKSON, E. *Childhood and Society.* New York: W. W. Norton, 1963.

FREUD, S. *Three Essays on the Theory of Sexuality.* Edited by J. Strachey. New York: Basic Books, 1963.

FROMM, E. *The Art of Loving.* New York: Harper and Row, 1956.

GOLDENSON, R. *The Encyclopedia of Human Behavior: Psychology, Psychiatry, and Mental Health.* New York: Doubleday and Company, Inc., 1970.

GREER, G. *The Female Eunuch.* New York: Bantam Books, 1972.

GUILFORD, J. *The Nature of Human Intelligence.* New York: McGraw-Hill, 1967.

HARLOW, H. *Learning to Love.* San Francisco: Albion, 1971.

KLEMER, R. *Marriage and Family Relations.* New York: Harper and Row, 1970.

MCCLELLAND, D. *Assessing Human Motivation.* New York: General Learning Press, 1971.

MASLOW, A. *Motivation and Personality.* New York: Harper and Row, 1954.

MEERLOO, J. *Conversation and Communication.* New York: International Press, 1952.

REUBEN, D. *Everything You Always Wanted to Know About Sex but Were Afraid to Ask.* New York: David McKay, 1969.

TOFFLER, A. *Future Shock.* New York: Bantam Books, 1971.

ANSWER SHEET

Name ____________________ Date ____________________

Yes ? No

1. ○ ○ ○
2. ○ ○ ○
3. ○ ○ ○
4. ○ ○ ○
5. ○ ○ ○
6. ○ ○ ○
7. ○ ○ ○
8. ○ ○ ○
9. ○ ○ ○
10. ○ ○ ○
11. ○ ○ ○
12. ○ ○ ○
13. ○ ○ ○
14. ○ ○ ○
15. ○ ○ ○
16. ○ ○ ○
17 ○ ○ ○
18. ○ ○ ○
19. ○ ○ ○
20. ○ ○ ○
21. ○ ○ ○
22. ○ ○ ○
23. ○ ○ ○
24. ○ ○ ○
25. ○ ○ ○
26. ○ ○ ○
27. ○ ○ ○
28. ○ ○ ○
29. ○ ○ ○
30. ○ ○ ○
31. ○ ○ ○
32. ○ ○ ○
33. ○ ○ ○
34. ○ ○ ○

Yes ? No

35. ○ ○ ○
36. ○ ○ ○
37. ○ ○ ○
38. ○ ○ ○
39. ○ ○ ○
40. ○ ○ ○
41. ○ ○ ○
42. ○ ○ ○
43. ○ ○ ○
44. ○ ○ ○
45. ○ ○ ○
46. ○ ○ ○
47. ○ ○ ○
48. ○ ○ ○
49. ○ ○ ○
50. ○ ○ ○

(1) (2) (3)

51. ○ ○ ○
52. ○ ○ ○
53. ○ ○ ○
54. ○ ○ ○
55. ○ ○ ○
56. ○ ○ ○
57. ○ ○ ○
58. ○ ○ ○
59. ○ ○ ○
60. ○ ○ ○
61. ○ ○ ○
62. ○ ○ ○
63. ○ ○ ○

Yes ? No

64. ○ ○ ○
65. ○ ○ ○
66. ○ ○ ○

Yes ? No

67. ○ ○ ○
68. ○ ○ ○
69. ○ ○ ○
70. ○ ○ ○
71. ○ ○ ○
72. ○ ○ ○
73. ○ ○ ○
74. ○ ○ ○
75. ○ ○ ○
76. ○ ○ ○
77. ○ ○ ○
78. ○ ○ ○
79. ○ ○ ○
80. ○ ○ ○
81. ○ ○ ○
82. ○ ○ ○
83. ○ ○ ○
84. ○ ○ ○
85. ○ ○ ○
86. ○ ○ ○
87. ○ ○ ○
88. ○ ○ ○
89. ○ ○ ○
90. ○ ○ ○
91 ○ ○ ○
92. ○ ○ ○
93. ○ ○ ○
94. ○ ○ ○
95. ○ ○ ○
96. ○ ○ ○
97. ○ ○ ○
98. ○ ○ ○
99. ○ ○ ○

Yes ? No

100. ○ ○ ○
101. ○ ○ ○
102. ○ ○ ○
103. ○ ○ ○
104. ○ ○ ○
105. ○ ○ ○
106. ○ ○ ○
107. ○ ○ ○
108. ○ ○ ○
109. ○ ○ ○
110. ○ ○ ○
111. ○ ○ ○
112. ○ ○ ○
113. ○ ○ ○
114. ○ ○ ○
115. ○ ○ ○
116. ○ ○ ○
117. ○ ○ ○
118. ○ ○ ○
119. ○ ○ ○
120. ○ ○ ○
121. ○ ○ ○
122. ○ ○ ○
123. ○ ○ ○
124. ○ ○ ○
125. ○ ○ ○
126. ○ ○ ○
127. ○ ○ ○
128. ○ ○ ○
129. ○ ○ ○
130. ○ ○ ○
141. ○ ○ ○
132. ○ ○ ○
133. ○ ○ ○
134. ○ ○ ○

Yes ? No

135. ○ ○ ○
136. ○ ○ ○
137. ○ ○ ○
138. ○ ○ ○
139. ○ ○ ○
140. ○ ○ ○
141. ○ ○ ○
142. ○ ○ ○
143. ○ ○ ○
144. ○ ○ ○
145. ○ ○ ○
146. ○ ○ ○
147. ○ ○ ○
148. ○ ○ ○
149. ○ ○ ○
150. ○ ○ ○
151. ○ ○ ○
152. ○ ○ ○

(1) (2) (3)

153. ○ ○ ○
154. ○ ○ ○
155. ○ ○ ○
156. ○ ○ ○
157. ○ ○ ○
158. ○ ○ ○
159. ○ ○ ○
100. ○ ○ ○
181. ○ ○ ○
162. ○ ○ ○
163. ○ ○ ○
164. ○ ○ ○
165. ○ ○ ○
166. ○ ○ ○

Yes ? No

167. ○ ○ ○
168. ○ ○ ○
169. ○ ○ ○
170. ○ ○ ○
171. ○ ○ ○
172. ○ ○ ○
173. ○ ○ ○
174. ○ ○ ○
175. ○ ○ ○
176. ○ ○ ○
177. ○ ○ ○
178. ○ ○ ○
179. ○ ○ ○
180. ○ ○ ○
181. ○ ○ ○
182. ○ ○ ○
183. ○ ○ ○
184. ○ ○ ○
185. ○ ○ ○
186. ○ ○ ○
187. ○ ○ ○
188. ○ ○ ○
189. ○ ○ ○
190. ○ ○ ○
181. ○ ○ ○
192. ○ ○ ○
193. ○ ○ ○
194. ○ ○ ○
195. ○ ○ ○
196. ○ ○ ○
197. ○ ○ ○
198. ○ ○ ○
199. ○ ○ ○
200. ○ ○ ○

Yes ? No

201. ○ ○ ○
202. ○ ○ ○
203. ○ ○ ○
204. ○ ○ ○
205. ○ ○ ○
206. ○ ○ ○
207. ○ ○ ○
208. ○ ○ ○

A
B
C
D
E
F

ANSWER SHEET

Name ______________________ Date ______________________

Yes ? No

1. ○ ○ ○
2. ○ ○ ○
3. ○ ○ ○
4. ○ ○ ○
5. ○ ○ ○
6. ○ ○ ○
7. ○ ○ ○
8. ○ ○ ○
9. ○ ○ ○
10. ○ ○ ○
11. ○ ○ ○
12. ○ ○ ○
13. ○ ○ ○
14. ○ ○ ○
15. ○ ○ ○
16. ○ ○ ○
17. ○ ○ ○
18. ○ ○ ○
19. ○ ○ ○
20. ○ ○ ○
21. ○ ○ ○
22. ○ ○ ○
23. ○ ○ ○
24. ○ ○ ○
25. ○ ○ ○
26. ○ ○ ○
27. ○ ○ ○
28. ○ ○ ○
29. ○ ○ ○
30. ○ ○ ○
31. ○ ○ ○
32. ○ ○ ○
33. ○ ○ ○
34. ○ ○ ○

Yes ? No

35. ○ ○ ○
36. ○ ○ ○
37. ○ ○ ○
38. ○ ○ ○
39. ○ ○ ○
40. ○ ○ ○
41. ○ ○ ○
42. ○ ○ ○
43. ○ ○ ○
44. ○ ○ ○
45. ○ ○ ○
46. ○ ○ ○
47. ○ ○ ○
48. ○ ○ ○
49. ○ ○ ○
50. ○ ○ ○

(1) (2) (3)

51. ○ ○ ○
52. ○ ○ ○
53. ○ ○ ○
54. ○ ○ ○
55. ○ ○ ○
56. ○ ○ ○
57. ○ ○ ○
58. ○ ○ ○
59. ○ ○ ○
60. ○ ○ ○
61. ○ ○ ○
62. ○ ○ ○
63. ○ ○ ○

Yes ? No

64. ○ ○ ○
65. ○ ○ ○
66. ○ ○ ○

Yes ? No

67. ○ ○ ○
68. ○ ○ ○
69. ○ ○ ○
70. ○ ○ ○
71. ○ ○ ○
72. ○ ○ ○
73. ○ ○ ○
74. ○ ○ ○
75. ○ ○ ○
76. ○ ○ ○
77. ○ ○ ○
78. ○ ○ ○
79. ○ ○ ○
80. ○ ○ ○
81. ○ ○ ○
82. ○ ○ ○
83. ○ ○ ○
84. ○ ○ ○
85. ○ ○ ○
86. ○ ○ ○
87. ○ ○ ○
88. ○ ○ ○
89. ○ ○ ○
90. ○ ○ ○
91. ○ ○ ○
92. ○ ○ ○
93. ○ ○ ○
94. ○ ○ ○
95. ○ ○ ○
96. ○ ○ ○
97. ○ ○ ○
98. ○ ○ ○
99. ○ ○ ○

Yes ? No

100. ○ ○ ○
101. ○ ○ ○
102. ○ ○ ○
103. ○ ○ ○
104. ○ ○ ○
105. ○ ○ ○
106. ○ ○ ○
107. ○ ○ ○
108. ○ ○ ○
109. ○ ○ ○
110. ○ ○ ○
111. ○ ○ ○
112. ○ ○ ○
113. ○ ○ ○
114. ○ ○ ○
115. ○ ○ ○
116. ○ ○ ○
117. ○ ○ ○
118. ○ ○ ○
119. ○ ○ ○
120. ○ ○ ○
121. ○ ○ ○
122. ○ ○ ○
123. ○ ○ ○
124. ○ ○ ○
125. ○ ○ ○
126. ○ ○ ○
127. ○ ○ ○
128. ○ ○ ○
129. ○ ○ ○
130. ○ ○ ○
131. ○ ○ ○
132. ○ ○ ○
133. ○ ○ ○
134. ○ ○ ○

Yes ? No

135. ○ ○ ○
136. ○ ○ ○
137. ○ ○ ○
138. ○ ○ ○
139. ○ ○ ○
140. ○ ○ ○
141. ○ ○ ○
142. ○ ○ ○
143. ○ ○ ○
144. ○ ○ ○
145. ○ ○ ○
146. ○ ○ ○
147. ○ ○ ○
148. ○ ○ ○
149. ○ ○ ○
150. ○ ○ ○
151. ○ ○ ○
152. ○ ○ ○

(1) (2) (3)

153. ○ ○ ○
154. ○ ○ ○
155. ○ ○ ○
156. ○ ○ ○
157. ○ ○ ○
158. ○ ○ ○
159. ○ ○ ○
160. ○ ○ ○
161. ○ ○ ○
162. ○ ○ ○
163. ○ ○ ○
164. ○ ○ ○
165. ○ ○ ○
166. ○ ○ ○

Yes ? No

167. ○ ○ ○
168. ○ ○ ○
169. ○ ○ ○
170. ○ ○ ○
171. ○ ○ ○
172. ○ ○ ○
173. ○ ○ ○
174. ○ ○ ○
175. ○ ○ ○
176. ○ ○ ○
177. ○ ○ ○
178. ○ ○ ○
179. ○ ○ ○
180. ○ ○ ○
181. ○ ○ ○
182. ○ ○ ○
183. ○ ○ ○
184. ○ ○ ○
185. ○ ○ ○
186. ○ ○ ○
187. ○ ○ ○
188. ○ ○ ○
189. ○ ○ ○
190. ○ ○ ○
191. ○ ○ ○
192. ○ ○ ○
193. ○ ○ ○
194. ○ ○ ○
195. ○ ○ ○
196. ○ ○ ○
197. ○ ○ ○
198. ○ ○ ○
199. ○ ○ ○
200. ○ ○ ○

Yes ? No

201. ○ ○ ○
202. ○ ○ ○
203. ○ ○ ○
204. ○ ○ ○
205. ○ ○ ○
206. ○ ○ ○
207. ○ ○ ○
208. ○ ○ ○

A
B
C
D
E
F

ANSWER SHEET

Name ____________ Date ____________

Yes ? No

1. ○ ○ ○
2. ○ ○ ○
3. ○ ○ ○
4. ○ ○ ○
5. ○ ○ ○
6. ○ ○ ○
7. ○ ○ ○
8. ○ ○ ○
9. ○ ○ ○
10. ○ ○ ○
11. ○ ○ ○
12. ○ ○ ○
13. ○ ○ ○
14. ○ ○ ○
15. ○ ○ ○
16. ○ ○ ○
17. ○ ○ ○
18. ○ ○ ○
19. ○ ○ ○
20. ○ ○ ○
21. ○ ○ ○
22. ○ ○ ○
23. ○ ○ ○
24. ○ ○ ○
25. ○ ○ ○
26. ○ ○ ○
27. ○ ○ ○
28. ○ ○ ○
29. ○ ○ ○
30. ○ ○ ○
31. ○ ○ ○
32. ○ ○ ○
33. ○ ○ ○
34. ○ ○ ○

Yes ? No

35. ○ ○ ○
36. ○ ○ ○
37. ○ ○ ○
38. ○ ○ ○
39. ○ ○ ○
40. ○ ○ ○
41. ○ ○ ○
42. ○ ○ ○
43. ○ ○ ○
44. ○ ○ ○
45. ○ ○ ○
46. ○ ○ ○
47. ○ ○ ○
48. ○ ○ ○
49. ○ ○ ○
50. ○ ○ ○

(1) (2) (3)

51. ○ ○ ○
52. ○ ○ ○
53. ○ ○ ○
54. ○ ○ ○
55. ○ ○ ○
56. ○ ○ ○
57. ○ ○ ○
58. ○ ○ ○
59. ○ ○ ○
60. ○ ○ ○
61. ○ ○ ○
62. ○ ○ ○
63. ○ ○ ○

Yes ? No

64. ○ ○ ○
65. ○ ○ ○
66. ○ ○ ○

Yes ? No

67. ○ ○ ○
68. ○ ○ ○
69. ○ ○ ○
70. ○ ○ ○
71. ○ ○ ○
72. ○ ○ ○
73. ○ ○ ○
74. ○ ○ ○
75. ○ ○ ○
76. ○ ○ ○
77. ○ ○ ○
78. ○ ○ ○
79. ○ ○ ○
80. ○ ○ ○
81. ○ ○ ○
82. ○ ○ ○
83. ○ ○ ○
84. ○ ○ ○
85. ○ ○ ○
86. ○ ○ ○
87. ○ ○ ○
88. ○ ○ ○
89. ○ ○ ○
90. ○ ○ ○
91 ○ ○ ○
92. ○ ○ ○
93. ○ ○ ○
94. ○ ○ ○
95. ○ ○ ○
96. ○ ○ ○
97. ○ ○ ○
98. ○ ○ ○
99. ○ ○ ○

Yes ? No

100. ○ ○ ○
101. ○ ○ ○
102. ○ ○ ○
103. ○ ○ ○
104. ○ ○ ○
105. ○ ○ ○
106. ○ ○ ○
107. ○ ○ ○
108. ○ ○ ○
109. ○ ○ ○
110. ○ ○ ○
111. ○ ○ ○
112. ○ ○ ○
113. ○ ○ ○
114. ○ ○ ○
115. ○ ○ ○
116. ○ ○ ○
117. ○ ○ ○
118. ○ ○ ○
119. ○ ○ ○
120. ○ ○ ○
121. ○ ○ ○
122. ○ ○ ○
123. ○ ○ ○
124. ○ ○ ○
125. ○ ○ ○
126. ○ ○ ○
127. ○ ○ ○
128. ○ ○ ○
129. ○ ○ ○
130. ○ ○ ○
141. ○ ○ ○
132. ○ ○ ○
133. ○ ○ ○
134. ○ ○ ○

Yes ? No

135. ○ ○ ○
136 ○ ○ ○
137. ○ ○ ○
138. ○ ○ ○
139. ○ ○ ○
140. ○ ○ ○
141. ○ ○ ○
142. ○ ○ ○
143. ○ ○ ○
144. ○ ○ ○
145. ○ ○ ○
146. ○ ○ ○
147. ○ ○ ○
148. ○ ○ ○
149. ○ ○ ○
160. ○ ○ ○
151. ○ ○ ○
152. ○ ○ ○

(1) (2) (3)

153. ○ ○ ○
154. ○ ○ ○
166. ○ ○ ○
156. ○ ○ ○
157. ○ ○ ○
158. ○ ○ ○
159. ○ ○ ○
160. ○ ○ ○
161. ○ ○ ○
162. ○ ○ ○
163. ○ ○ ○
164. ○ ○ ○
165. ○ ○ ○
166. ○ ○ ○

Yes ? No

167. ○ ○ ○
168. ○ ○ ○
169. ○ ○ ○
170. ○ ○ ○
171. ○ ○ ○
172. ○ ○ ○
173. ○ ○ ○
174. ○ ○ ○
175. ○ ○ ○
176. ○ ○ ○
177. ○ ○ ○
178. ○ ○ ○
179. ○ ○ ○
180. ○ ○ ○
181. ○ ○ ○
182. ○ ○ ○
183. ○ ○ ○
184. ○ ○ ○
185. ○ ○ ○
186. ○ ○ ○
187. ○ ○ ○
188. ○ ○ ○
189. ○ ○ ○
190. ○ ○ ○
191. ○ ○ ○
192. ○ ○ ○
193. ○ ○ ○
194. ○ ○ ○
195. ○ ○ ○
196. ○ ○ ○
197. ○ ○ ○
198. ○ ○ ○
199. ○ ○ ○
200. ○ ○ ○

Yes ? No

201. ○ ○ ○
202. ○ ○ ○
203. ○ ○ ○
204. ○ ○ ○
205. ○ ○ ○
206. ○ ○ ○
207. ○ ○ ○
208. ○ ○ ○

A
B
C
D
E
F

ANSWER SHEET

Name ____________________ Date ____________________

Yes ? No

1. ○ ○ ○
2. ○ ○ ○
3. ○ ○ ○
4. ○ ○ ○
5. ○ ○ ○
6. ○ ○ ○
7. ○ ○ ○
8. ○ ○ ○
9. ○ ○ ○
10. ○ ○ ○
11. ○ ○ ○
12. ○ ○ ○
13. ○ ○ ○
14. ○ ○ ○
15. ○ ○ ○
16. ○ ○ ○
17. ○ ○ ○
18. ○ ○ ○
19. ○ ○ ○
20. ○ ○ ○
21. ○ ○ ○
22. ○ ○ ○
23. ○ ○ ○
24. ○ ○ ○
25. ○ ○ ○
26. ○ ○ ○
27. ○ ○ ○
28. ○ ○ ○
29. ○ ○ ○
30. ○ ○ ○
31. ○ ○ ○
32. ○ ○ ○
33. ○ ○ ○
34. ○ ○ ○

Yes ? No

35. ○ ○ ○
36. ○ ○ ○
37. ○ ○ ○
38. ○ ○ ○
39. ○ ○ ○
40. ○ ○ ○
41. ○ ○ ○
42. ○ ○ ○
43. ○ ○ ○
44. ○ ○ ○
45. ○ ○ ○
46. ○ ○ ○
47. ○ ○ ○
48. ○ ○ ○
49. ○ ○ ○
50. ○ ○ ○

(1) (2) (3)

51. ○ ○ ○
52. ○ ○ ○
53. ○ ○ ○
54. ○ ○ ○
55. ○ ○ ○
56. ○ ○ ○
57. ○ ○ ○
58. ○ ○ ○
59. ○ ○ ○
60. ○ ○ ○
61. ○ ○ ○
62. ○ ○ ○
63. ○ ○ ○

Yes ? No

64. ○ ○ ○
65. ○ ○ ○
66. ○ ○ ○

Yes ? No

67. ○ ○ ○
68. ○ ○ ○
69. ○ ○ ○
70. ○ ○ ○
71. ○ ○ ○
72. ○ ○ ○
73. ○ ○ ○
74. ○ ○ ○
75. ○ ○ ○
76. ○ ○ ○
77. ○ ○ ○
78. ○ ○ ○
79. ○ ○ ○
80. ○ ○ ○
81. ○ ○ ○
82. ○ ○ ○
83. ○ ○ ○
84. ○ ○ ○
85. ○ ○ ○
86. ○ ○ ○
87. ○ ○ ○
88. ○ ○ ○
89. ○ ○ ○
90. ○ ○ ○
91. ○ ○ ○
92. ○ ○ ○
93. ○ ○ ○
94. ○ ○ ○
95. ○ ○ ○
96. ○ ○ ○
97. ○ ○ ○
98. ○ ○ ○
99. ○ ○ ○

Yes ? No

100. ○ ○ ○
101. ○ ○ ○
102. ○ ○ ○
103. ○ ○ ○
104. ○ ○ ○
105. ○ ○ ○
106. ○ ○ ○
107. ○ ○ ○
108. ○ ○ ○
109. ○ ○ ○
110. ○ ○ ○
111. ○ ○ ○
112. ○ ○ ○
113. ○ ○ ○
114. ○ ○ ○
115. ○ ○ ○
116. ○ ○ ○
117. ○ ○ ○
118. ○ ○ ○
119. ○ ○ ○
120. ○ ○ ○
121. ○ ○ ○
122. ○ ○ ○
123. ○ ○ ○
124. ○ ○ ○
125. ○ ○ ○
126. ○ ○ ○
127. ○ ○ ○
128. ○ ○ ○
129. ○ ○ ○
130. ○ ○ ○
141. ○ ○ ○
132. ○ ○ ○
133. ○ ○ ○
134. ○ ○ ○

Yes ? No

135. ○ ○ ○
136. ○ ○ ○
137. ○ ○ ○
138. ○ ○ ○
139. ○ ○ ○
140. ○ ○ ○
141. ○ ○ ○
142. ○ ○ ○
143. ○ ○ ○
144. ○ ○ ○
145. ○ ○ ○
146. ○ ○ ○
147. ○ ○ ○
148. ○ ○ ○
149. ○ ○ ○
150. ○ ○ ○
151. ○ ○ ○
152. ○ ○ ○

(1) (2) (3)

153. ○ ○ ○
154. ○ ○ ○
155. ○ ○ ○
156. ○ ○ ○
157. ○ ○ ○
158. ○ ○ ○
159. ○ ○ ○
160. ○ ○ ○
161. ○ ○ ○
162. ○ ○ ○
163. ○ ○ ○
164. ○ ○ ○
165. ○ ○ ○
166. ○ ○ ○

Yes ? No

167. ○ ○ ○
168. ○ ○ ○
169. ○ ○ ○
170. ○ ○ ○
171. ○ ○ ○
172. ○ ○ ○
173. ○ ○ ○
174. ○ ○ ○
175. ○ ○ ○
176. ○ ○ ○
177. ○ ○ ○
178. ○ ○ ○
179. ○ ○ ○
180. ○ ○ ○
181. ○ ○ ○
182. ○ ○ ○
183. ○ ○ ○
184. ○ ○ ○
185. ○ ○ ○
186. ○ ○ ○
187. ○ ○ ○
188. ○ ○ ○
189. ○ ○ ○
190. ○ ○ ○
191. ○ ○ ○
192. ○ ○ ○
193. ○ ○ ○
194. ○ ○ ○
195. ○ ○ ○
196. ○ ○ ○
197. ○ ○ ○
198. ○ ○ ○
199. ○ ○ ○
200. ○ ○ ○

Yes ? No

201. ○ ○ ○
202. ○ ○ ○
203. ○ ○ ○
204. ○ ○ ○
205. ○ ○ ○
206. ○ ○ ○
207. ○ ○ ○
208. ○ ○ ○

A
B
C
D
E
F

ANSWER SHEET

Name ____________________ Date ____________________

Yes ? No

1. ○ ○ ○
2. ○ ○ ○
3. ○ ○ ○
4. ○ ○ ○
5. ○ ○ ○
6. ○ ○ ○
7. ○ ○ ○
8. ○ ○ ○
9. ○ ○ ○
10. ○ ○ ○
11. ○ ○ ○
12. ○ ○ ○
13. ○ ○ ○
14. ○ ○ ○
15. ○ ○ ○
16. ○ ○ ○
17. ○ ○ ○
18. ○ ○ ○
19. ○ ○ ○
20. ○ ○ ○
21. ○ ○ ○
22. ○ ○ ○
23. ○ ○ ○
24. ○ ○ ○
25. ○ ○ ○
26. ○ ○ ○
27. ○ ○ ○
28. ○ ○ ○
29. ○ ○ ○
30. ○ ○ ○
31. ○ ○ ○
32. ○ ○ ○
33. ○ ○ ○
34. ○ ○ ○

Yes ? No

35. ○ ○ ○
36. ○ ○ ○
37. ○ ○ ○
38. ○ ○ ○
39. ○ ○ ○
40. ○ ○ ○
41. ○ ○ ○
42. ○ ○ ○
43. ○ ○ ○
44. ○ ○ ○
45. ○ ○ ○
46. ○ ○ ○
47. ○ ○ ○
48. ○ ○ ○
49. ○ ○ ○
50. ○ ○ ○

(1) (2) (3)

51. ○ ○ ○
52. ○ ○ ○
53. ○ ○ ○
54. ○ ○ ○
55. ○ ○ ○
56. ○ ○ ○
57. ○ ○ ○
58. ○ ○ ○
59. ○ ○ ○
60. ○ ○ ○
61. ○ ○ ○
62. ○ ○ ○
63. ○ ○ ○

Yes ? No

64. ○ ○ ○
65. ○ ○ ○
66. ○ ○ ○

Yes ? No

67. ○ ○ ○
68. ○ ○ ○
69. ○ ○ ○
70. ○ ○ ○
71. ○ ○ ○
72. ○ ○ ○
73. ○ ○ ○
74. ○ ○ ○
75. ○ ○ ○
76. ○ ○ ○
77. ○ ○ ○
78. ○ ○ ○
79. ○ ○ ○
80. ○ ○ ○
81. ○ ○ ○
82. ○ ○ ○
83. ○ ○ ○
84. ○ ○ ○
85. ○ ○ ○
86. ○ ○ ○
87. ○ ○ ○
88. ○ ○ ○
89. ○ ○ ○
90. ○ ○ ○
91. ○ ○ ○
92. ○ ○ ○
93. ○ ○ ○
94. ○ ○ ○
95. ○ ○ ○
96. ○ ○ ○
97. ○ ○ ○
98. ○ ○ ○
99. ○ ○ ○

Yes ? No

100. ○ ○ ○
101. ○ ○ ○
102. ○ ○ ○
103. ○ ○ ○
104. ○ ○ ○
105. ○ ○ ○
106. ○ ○ ○
107. ○ ○ ○
108. ○ ○ ○
109. ○ ○ ○
110. ○ ○ ○
111. ○ ○ ○
112. ○ ○ ○
113. ○ ○ ○
114. ○ ○ ○
115. ○ ○ ○
116. ○ ○ ○
117. ○ ○ ○
118. ○ ○ ○
119. ○ ○ ○
120. ○ ○ ○
121. ○ ○ ○
122. ○ ○ ○
123. ○ ○ ○
124. ○ ○ ○
125. ○ ○ ○
126. ○ ○ ○
127. ○ ○ ○
128. ○ ○ ○
129. ○ ○ ○
130. ○ ○ ○
141. ○ ○ ○
132. ○ ○ ○
133. ○ ○ ○
134. ○ ○ ○

Yes ? No

135. ○ ○ ○
136. ○ ○ ○
137. ○ ○ ○
138. ○ ○ ○
139. ○ ○ ○
140. ○ ○ ○
141. ○ ○ ○
142. ○ ○ ○
143. ○ ○ ○
144. ○ ○ ○
145. ○ ○ ○
146. ○ ○ ○
147. ○ ○ ○
148. ○ ○ ○
149. ○ ○ ○
150. ○ ○ ○
151. ○ ○ ○
152. ○ ○ ○

(1) (2) (3)

153. ○ ○ ○
154. ○ ○ ○
155. ○ ○ ○
156. ○ ○ ○
157. ○ ○ ○
158. ○ ○ ○
159. ○ ○ ○
160. ○ ○ ○
161. ○ ○ ○
162. ○ ○ ○
163. ○ ○ ○
164. ○ ○ ○
165. ○ ○ ○
166. ○ ○ ○

Yes ? No

167. ○ ○ ○
168. ○ ○ ○
169. ○ ○ ○
170. ○ ○ ○
171. ○ ○ ○
172. ○ ○ ○
173. ○ ○ ○
174. ○ ○ ○
175. ○ ○ ○
176. ○ ○ ○
177. ○ ○ ○
178. ○ ○ ○
179. ○ ○ ○
180. ○ ○ ○
181. ○ ○ ○
182. ○ ○ ○
183. ○ ○ ○
184. ○ ○ ○
185. ○ ○ ○
186. ○ ○ ○
187. ○ ○ ○
188. ○ ○ ○
189. ○ ○ ○
190. ○ ○ ○
191. ○ ○ ○
192. ○ ○ ○
193. ○ ○ ○
194. ○ ○ ○
195. ○ ○ ○
196. ○ ○ ○
197. ○ ○ ○
198. ○ ○ ○
199. ○ ○ ○
200. ○ ○ ○

Yes ? No

201. ○ ○ ○
202. ○ ○ ○
203. ○ ○ ○
204. ○ ○ ○
205. ○ ○ ○
206. ○ ○ ○
207. ○ ○ ○
208. ○ ○ ○

A
B
C
D
E
F

ANSWER SHEET

Name ____________________ Date ____________________

Yes ? No
1. ○ ○ ○
2. ○ ○ ○
3. ○ ○ ○
4. ○ ○ ○
5. ○ ○ ○
6. ○ ○ ○
7. ○ ○ ○
8. ○ ○ ○
9. ○ ○ ○
10. ○ ○ ○
11. ○ ○ ○
12. ○ ○ ○
13. ○ ○ ○
14. ○ ○ ○
15. ○ ○ ○
16. ○ ○ ○
17. ○ ○ ○
18. ○ ○ ○
19. ○ ○ ○
20. ○ ○ ○
21. ○ ○ ○
22. ○ ○ ○
23. ○ ○ ○
24. ○ ○ ○
25. ○ ○ ○
26. ○ ○ ○
27. ○ ○ ○
28. ○ ○ ○
29. ○ ○ ○
30. ○ ○ ○
31. ○ ○ ○
32. ○ ○ ○
33. ○ ○ ○
34. ○ ○ ○

Yes ? No
35. ○ ○ ○
36. ○ ○ ○
37. ○ ○ ○
38. ○ ○ ○
39. ○ ○ ○
40. ○ ○ ○
41. ○ ○ ○
42. ○ ○ ○
43. ○ ○ ○
44. ○ ○ ○
45. ○ ○ ○
46. ○ ○ ○
47. ○ ○ ○
48. ○ ○ ○
49. ○ ○ ○
50. ○ ○ ○

(1) (2) (3)
51. ○ ○ ○
52. ○ ○ ○
53. ○ ○ ○
54. ○ ○ ○
55. ○ ○ ○
56. ○ ○ ○
57. ○ ○ ○
58. ○ ○ ○
59. ○ ○ ○
60. ○ ○ ○
61. ○ ○ ○
62. ○ ○ ○
63. ○ ○ ○

Yes ? No
64. ○ ○ ○
65. ○ ○ ○
66. ○ ○ ○

Yes ? No
67. ○ ○ ○
68. ○ ○ ○
69. ○ ○ ○
70. ○ ○ ○
71. ○ ○ ○
72. ○ ○ ○
73. ○ ○ ○
74. ○ ○ ○
75. ○ ○ ○
76. ○ ○ ○
77. ○ ○ ○
78. ○ ○ ○
79. ○ ○ ○
80. ○ ○ ○
81. ○ ○ ○
82. ○ ○ ○
83. ○ ○ ○
84. ○ ○ ○
85. ○ ○ ○
86. ○ ○ ○
87. ○ ○ ○
88. ○ ○ ○
89. ○ ○ ○
90. ○ ○ ○
91. ○ ○ ○
92. ○ ○ ○
93. ○ ○ ○
94. ○ ○ ○
95. ○ ○ ○
96. ○ ○ ○
97. ○ ○ ○
98. ○ ○ ○
99. ○ ○ ○

Yes ? No
100. ○ ○ ○
101. ○ ○ ○
102. ○ ○ ○
103. ○ ○ ○
104. ○ ○ ○
105. ○ ○ ○
106. ○ ○ ○
107. ○ ○ ○
108. ○ ○ ○
109. ○ ○ ○
110. ○ ○ ○
111. ○ ○ ○
112. ○ ○ ○
113. ○ ○ ○
114. ○ ○ ○
115. ○ ○ ○
116. ○ ○ ○
117. ○ ○ ○
118. ○ ○ ○
119. ○ ○ ○
120. ○ ○ ○
121. ○ ○ ○
122. ○ ○ ○
123. ○ ○ ○
124. ○ ○ ○
125. ○ ○ ○
126. ○ ○ ○
127. ○ ○ ○
128. ○ ○ ○
129. ○ ○ ○
130. ○ ○ ○
141. ○ ○ ○
132. ○ ○ ○
133. ○ ○ ○
134. ○ ○ ○

Yes ? No
135. ○ ○ ○
136. ○ ○ ○
137. ○ ○ ○
138. ○ ○ ○
139. ○ ○ ○
140. ○ ○ ○
141. ○ ○ ○
142. ○ ○ ○
143. ○ ○ ○
144. ○ ○ ○
145. ○ ○ ○
146. ○ ○ ○
147. ○ ○ ○
148. ○ ○ ○
149. ○ ○ ○
150. ○ ○ ○
151. ○ ○ ○
152. ○ ○ ○

(1) (2) (3)
153. ○ ○ ○
154. ○ ○ ○
155. ○ ○ ○
156. ○ ○ ○
157. ○ ○ ○
158. ○ ○ ○
159. ○ ○ ○
160. ○ ○ ○
161. ○ ○ ○
162. ○ ○ ○
163. ○ ○ ○
164. ○ ○ ○
165. ○ ○ ○
166. ○ ○ ○

Yes ? No
167. ○ ○ ○
168. ○ ○ ○
169. ○ ○ ○
170. ○ ○ ○
171. ○ ○ ○
172. ○ ○ ○
173. ○ ○ ○
174. ○ ○ ○
175. ○ ○ ○
176. ○ ○ ○
177. ○ ○ ○
178. ○ ○ ○
179. ○ ○ ○
180. ○ ○ ○
181. ○ ○ ○
182. ○ ○ ○
183. ○ ○ ○
184. ○ ○ ○
185. ○ ○ ○
186. ○ ○ ○
187. ○ ○ ○
188. ○ ○ ○
189. ○ ○ ○
190. ○ ○ ○
191. ○ ○ ○
192. ○ ○ ○
193. ○ ○ ○
194. ○ ○ ○
195. ○ ○ ○
196. ○ ○ ○
197. ○ ○ ○
198. ○ ○ ○
199. ○ ○ ○
200. ○ ○ ○

Yes ? No
201. ○ ○ ○
202. ○ ○ ○
203. ○ ○ ○
204. ○ ○ ○
205. ○ ○ ○
206. ○ ○ ○
207. ○ ○ ○
208. ○ ○ ○

A
B
C
D
E
F

ANSWER SHEET

Name ______________________ Date ______________________

Yes ? No

1. ○ ○ ○
2. ○ ○ ○
3. ○ ○ ○
4. ○ ○ ○
5. ○ ○ ○
6. ○ ○ ○
7. ○ ○ ○
8. ○ ○ ○
9. ○ ○ ○
10. ○ ○ ○
11. ○ ○ ○
12. ○ ○ ○
13. ○ ○ ○
14. ○ ○ ○
15. ○ ○ ○
16. ○ ○ ○
17. ○ ○ ○
18. ○ ○ ○
19. ○ ○ ○
20. ○ ○ ○
21. ○ ○ ○
22. ○ ○ ○
23. ○ ○ ○
24. ○ ○ ○
25. ○ ○ ○
26. ○ ○ ○
27. ○ ○ ○
28. ○ ○ ○
29. ○ ○ ○
30. ○ ○ ○
31. ○ ○ ○
32. ○ ○ ○
33. ○ ○ ○
34. ○ ○ ○

Yes ? No

35. ○ ○ ○
36. ○ ○ ○
37. ○ ○ ○
38. ○ ○ ○
39. ○ ○ ○
40. ○ ○ ○
41. ○ ○ ○
42. ○ ○ ○
43. ○ ○ ○
44. ○ ○ ○
45. ○ ○ ○
46. ○ ○ ○
47. ○ ○ ○
48. ○ ○ ○
49. ○ ○ ○
50. ○ ○ ○

(1) (2) (3)

51. ○ ○ ○
52. ○ ○ ○
53. ○ ○ ○
54. ○ ○ ○
55. ○ ○ ○
56. ○ ○ ○
57. ○ ○ ○
58. ○ ○ ○
59. ○ ○ ○
60. ○ ○ ○
61. ○ ○ ○
62. ○ ○ ○
63. ○ ○ ○

Yes ? No

64. ○ ○ ○
65. ○ ○ ○
66. ○ ○ ○

Yes ? No

67. ○ ○ ○
68. ○ ○ ○
69. ○ ○ ○
70. ○ ○ ○
71. ○ ○ ○
72. ○ ○ ○
73. ○ ○ ○
74. ○ ○ ○
75. ○ ○ ○
76. ○ ○ ○
77. ○ ○ ○
78. ○ ○ ○
79. ○ ○ ○
80. ○ ○ ○
81. ○ ○ ○
82. ○ ○ ○
83. ○ ○ ○
84. ○ ○ ○
85. ○ ○ ○
86. ○ ○ ○
87. ○ ○ ○
88. ○ ○ ○
89. ○ ○ ○
90. ○ ○ ○
91. ○ ○ ○
92. ○ ○ ○
93. ○ ○ ○
94. ○ ○ ○
95. ○ ○ ○
96. ○ ○ ○
97. ○ ○ ○
98. ○ ○ ○
99. ○ ○ ○

Yes ? No

100. ○ ○ ○
101. ○ ○ ○
102. ○ ○ ○
103. ○ ○ ○
104. ○ ○ ○
105. ○ ○ ○
106. ○ ○ ○
107. ○ ○ ○
108. ○ ○ ○
109. ○ ○ ○
110. ○ ○ ○
111. ○ ○ ○
112. ○ ○ ○
113. ○ ○ ○
114. ○ ○ ○
115. ○ ○ ○
116. ○ ○ ○
117. ○ ○ ○
118. ○ ○ ○
119. ○ ○ ○
120. ○ ○ ○
121. ○ ○ ○
122. ○ ○ ○
123. ○ ○ ○
124. ○ ○ ○
125. ○ ○ ○
126. ○ ○ ○
127. ○ ○ ○
128. ○ ○ ○
129. ○ ○ ○
130. ○ ○ ○
141. ○ ○ ○
132. ○ ○ ○
133. ○ ○ ○
134. ○ ○ ○

Yes ? No

135. ○ ○ ○
136. ○ ○ ○
137. ○ ○ ○
138. ○ ○ ○
139. ○ ○ ○
140. ○ ○ ○
141. ○ ○ ○
142. ○ ○ ○
143. ○ ○ ○
144. ○ ○ ○
145. ○ ○ ○
146. ○ ○ ○
147. ○ ○ ○
148. ○ ○ ○
149. ○ ○ ○
150. ○ ○ ○
151. ○ ○ ○
152. ○ ○ ○

(1) (2) (3)

153. ○ ○ ○
154. ○ ○ ○
155. ○ ○ ○
156. ○ ○ ○
157. ○ ○ ○
158. ○ ○ ○
159. ○ ○ ○
160. ○ ○ ○
161. ○ ○ ○
162. ○ ○ ○
163. ○ ○ ○
164. ○ ○ ○
165. ○ ○ ○
166. ○ ○ ○

Yes ? No

167. ○ ○ ○
168. ○ ○ ○
169. ○ ○ ○
170. ○ ○ ○
171. ○ ○ ○
172. ○ ○ ○
173. ○ ○ ○
174. ○ ○ ○
175. ○ ○ ○
176. ○ ○ ○
177. ○ ○ ○
178. ○ ○ ○
179. ○ ○ ○
180. ○ ○ ○
181. ○ ○ ○
182. ○ ○ ○
183. ○ ○ ○
184. ○ ○ ○
185. ○ ○ ○
186. ○ ○ ○
187. ○ ○ ○
188. ○ ○ ○
189. ○ ○ ○
190. ○ ○ ○
191. ○ ○ ○
192. ○ ○ ○
193. ○ ○ ○
194. ○ ○ ○
195. ○ ○ ○
196. ○ ○ ○
197. ○ ○ ○
198. ○ ○ ○
199. ○ ○ ○
200. ○ ○ ○

Yes ? No

201. ○ ○ ○
202. ○ ○ ○
203. ○ ○ ○
204. ○ ○ ○
205. ○ ○ ○
206. ○ ○ ○
207. ○ ○ ○
208. ○ ○ ○

A
B
C
D
E
F

ANSWER SHEET

Name ____________________ Date ____________________

Yes ? No

1. ○ ○ ○
2. ○ ○ ○
3. ○ ○ ○
4. ○ ○ ○
5. ○ ○ ○
6. ○ ○ ○
7. ○ ○ ○
8. ○ ○ ○
9. ○ ○ ○
10. ○ ○ ○
11. ○ ○ ○
12. ○ ○ ○
13. ○ ○ ○
14. ○ ○ ○
15. ○ ○ ○
16. ○ ○ ○
17. ○ ○ ○
18. ○ ○ ○
19. ○ ○ ○
20. ○ ○ ○
21. ○ ○ ○
22. ○ ○ ○
23. ○ ○ ○
24. ○ ○ ○
25. ○ ○ ○
26. ○ ○ ○
27. ○ ○ ○
28. ○ ○ ○
29. ○ ○ ○
30. ○ ○ ○
31. ○ ○ ○
32. ○ ○ ○
33. ○ ○ ○
34. ○ ○ ○

Yes ? No

35. ○ ○ ○
36. ○ ○ ○
37. ○ ○ ○
38. ○ ○ ○
39. ○ ○ ○
40. ○ ○ ○
41. ○ ○ ○
42. ○ ○ ○
43. ○ ○ ○
44. ○ ○ ○
45. ○ ○ ○
46. ○ ○ ○
47. ○ ○ ○
48. ○ ○ ○
49. ○ ○ ○
50. ○ ○ ○

(1) (2) (3)

51. ○ ○ ○
52. ○ ○ ○
53. ○ ○ ○
54. ○ ○ ○
55. ○ ○ ○
56. ○ ○ ○
57. ○ ○ ○
58. ○ ○ ○
59. ○ ○ ○
60. ○ ○ ○
61. ○ ○ ○
62. ○ ○ ○
63. ○ ○ ○

Yes ? No

64. ○ ○ ○
65. ○ ○ ○
66. ○ ○ ○

Yes ? No

67. ○ ○ ○
68. ○ ○ ○
69. ○ ○ ○
70. ○ ○ ○
71. ○ ○ ○
72. ○ ○ ○
73. ○ ○ ○
74. ○ ○ ○
75. ○ ○ ○
76. ○ ○ ○
77. ○ ○ ○
78. ○ ○ ○
79. ○ ○ ○
80. ○ ○ ○
81. ○ ○ ○
82. ○ ○ ○
83. ○ ○ ○
84. ○ ○ ○
85. ○ ○ ○
86. ○ ○ ○
87. ○ ○ ○
88. ○ ○ ○
89. ○ ○ ○
90. ○ ○ ○
91. ○ ○ ○
92. ○ ○ ○
93. ○ ○ ○
94. ○ ○ ○
95. ○ ○ ○
96. ○ ○ ○
97. ○ ○ ○
98. ○ ○ ○
99. ○ ○ ○

Yes ? No

100. ○ ○ ○
101. ○ ○ ○
102. ○ ○ ○
103. ○ ○ ○
104. ○ ○ ○
105. ○ ○ ○
106. ○ ○ ○
107. ○ ○ ○
108. ○ ○ ○
109. ○ ○ ○
110. ○ ○ ○
111. ○ ○ ○
112. ○ ○ ○
113. ○ ○ ○
114. ○ ○ ○
115. ○ ○ ○
116. ○ ○ ○
117. ○ ○ ○
118. ○ ○ ○
119. ○ ○ ○
120. ○ ○ ○
121. ○ ○ ○
122. ○ ○ ○
123. ○ ○ ○
124. ○ ○ ○
125. ○ ○ ○
126. ○ ○ ○
127. ○ ○ ○
128. ○ ○ ○
129. ○ ○ ○
130. ○ ○ ○
131. ○ ○ ○
132. ○ ○ ○
133. ○ ○ ○
134. ○ ○ ○

Yes ? No

135. ○ ○ ○
136. ○ ○ ○
137. ○ ○ ○
138. ○ ○ ○
139. ○ ○ ○
140. ○ ○ ○
141. ○ ○ ○
142. ○ ○ ○
143. ○ ○ ○
144. ○ ○ ○
145. ○ ○ ○
146. ○ ○ ○
147. ○ ○ ○
148. ○ ○ ○
149. ○ ○ ○
150. ○ ○ ○
151. ○ ○ ○
152. ○ ○ ○

(1) (2) (3)

153. ○ ○ ○
154. ○ ○ ○
155. ○ ○ ○
156. ○ ○ ○
157. ○ ○ ○
158. ○ ○ ○
159. ○ ○ ○
160. ○ ○ ○
161. ○ ○ ○
162. ○ ○ ○
163. ○ ○ ○
164. ○ ○ ○
165. ○ ○ ○
166. ○ ○ ○

Yes ? No

167. ○ ○ ○
168. ○ ○ ○
169. ○ ○ ○
170. ○ ○ ○
171. ○ ○ ○
172. ○ ○ ○
173. ○ ○ ○
174. ○ ○ ○
175. ○ ○ ○
176. ○ ○ ○
177. ○ ○ ○
178. ○ ○ ○
179. ○ ○ ○
180. ○ ○ ○
181. ○ ○ ○
182. ○ ○ ○
183. ○ ○ ○
184. ○ ○ ○
185. ○ ○ ○
186. ○ ○ ○
187. ○ ○ ○
188. ○ ○ ○
189. ○ ○ ○
190. ○ ○ ○
191. ○ ○ ○
192. ○ ○ ○
193. ○ ○ ○
194. ○ ○ ○
195. ○ ○ ○
196. ○ ○ ○
197. ○ ○ ○
198. ○ ○ ○
199. ○ ○ ○
200. ○ ○ ○

Yes ? No

201. ○ ○ ○
202. ○ ○ ○
203. ○ ○ ○
204. ○ ○ ○
205. ○ ○ ○
206. ○ ○ ○
207. ○ ○ ○
208. ○ ○ ○

A
B
C
D
E
F

ANSWER SHEET

Name ____________________ Date ____________________

Yes ? No

1. 2. 3. 4. 5. 6. 7. 8. 9. 10. 11. 12. 13. 14. 15. 16. 17. 18. 19. 20. 21. 22. 23. 24. 25. 26. 27. 28. 29. 30. 31. 32. 33. 34.

Yes ? No

35. 36. 37. 38. 39. 40. 41. 42. 43. 44. 45. 46. 47. 48. 49. 50.

(1) (2) (3)

51. 52. 53. 54. 55. 56. 57. 58. 59. 60. 61. 62. 63.

Yes ? No

64. 65. 66.

Yes ? No

67. 68. 69. 70. 71. 72. 73. 74. 75. 76. 77. 78. 79. 80. 81. 82. 83. 84. 85. 86. 87. 88. 89. 90. 91. 92. 93. 94. 95. 96. 97. 98. 99.

Yes ? No

100. 101. 102. 103. 104. 105. 106. 107. 108. 109. 110. 111. 112. 113. 114. 115. 116. 117. 118. 119. 120. 121. 122. 123. 124. 125. 126. 127. 128. 129. 130. 141. 132. 133. 134.

Yes ? No

135. 136. 137. 138. 139. 140. 141. 142. 143. 144. 145. 146. 147. 148. 149. 150. 151. 152.

(1) (2) (3)

153. 154. 155. 156. 157. 158. 159. 160. 161. 162. 163. 164. 165. 166.

Yes ? No

167. 168. 169. 170. 171. 172. 173. 174. 175. 176. 177. 178. 179. 180. 181. 182. 183. 184. 185. 186. 187. 188. 189. 190. 191. 192. 193. 194. 195. 196. 197. 198. 199. 200.

Yes ? No

201. 202. 203. 204. 205. 206. 207. 208.

A

B

C

D

E

F

ANSWER SHEET

Name ______________________ Date ______________________

Yes ? No

1. ○ ○ ○
2. ○ ○ ○
3. ○ ○ ○
4. ○ ○ ○
5. ○ ○ ○
6. ○ ○ ○
7. ○ ○ ○
8. ○ ○ ○
9. ○ ○ ○
10. ○ ○ ○
11. ○ ○ ○
12. ○ ○ ○
13. ○ ○ ○
14. ○ ○ ○
15. ○ ○ ○
16. ○ ○ ○
17. ○ ○ ○
18. ○ ○ ○
19. ○ ○ ○
20. ○ ○ ○
21. ○ ○ ○
22. ○ ○ ○
23. ○ ○ ○
24. ○ ○ ○
25. ○ ○ ○
26. ○ ○ ○
27. ○ ○ ○
28. ○ ○ ○
30. ○ ○ ○
30. ○ ○ ○
31. ○ ○ ○
32. ○ ○ ○
33. ○ ○ ○
34. ○ ○ ○

Yes ? No

35. ○ ○ ○
36. ○ ○ ○
37. ○ ○ ○
38. ○ ○ ○
39. ○ ○ ○
40. ○ ○ ○
41. ○ ○ ○
42. ○ ○ ○
43. ○ ○ ○
44. ○ ○ ○
45. ○ ○ ○
46. ○ ○ ○
47. ○ ○ ○
48. ○ ○ ○
49. ○ ○ ○
50. ○ ○ ○

(1) (2) (3)

51. ○ ○ ○
52. ○ ○ ○
53. ○ ○ ○
54. ○ ○ ○
55. ○ ○ ○
56. ○ ○ ○
57. ○ ○ ○
58. ○ ○ ○
59. ○ ○ ○
60. ○ ○ ○
61. ○ ○ ○
62. ○ ○ ○
63. ○ ○ ○

Yes ? No

64. ○ ○ ○
65. ○ ○ ○
66. ○ ○ ○

Yes ? No

67. ○ ○ ○
68. ○ ○ ○
69. ○ ○ ○
70. ○ ○ ○
71. ○ ○ ○
72. ○ ○ ○
73. ○ ○ ○
74. ○ ○ ○
75. ○ ○ ○
76. ○ ○ ○
77. ○ ○ ○
78. ○ ○ ○
79. ○ ○ ○
80. ○ ○ ○
81. ○ ○ ○
82. ○ ○ ○
83. ○ ○ ○
84. ○ ○ ○
85. ○ ○ ○
86. ○ ○ ○
87. ○ ○ ○
88. ○ ○ ○
89. ○ ○ ○
90. ○ ○ ○
91. ○ ○ ○
92. ○ ○ ○
93. ○ ○ ○
94. ○ ○ ○
95. ○ ○ ○
96. ○ ○ ○
97. ○ ○ ○
98. ○ ○ ○
99. ○ ○ ○

Yes ? No

100. ○ ○ ○
101. ○ ○ ○
102. ○ ○ ○
103. ○ ○ ○
104. ○ ○ ○
105. ○ ○ ○
106. ○ ○ ○
107. ○ ○ ○
108. ○ ○ ○
109. ○ ○ ○
110. ○ ○ ○
111. ○ ○ ○
112. ○ ○ ○
113. ○ ○ ○
114. ○ ○ ○
115. ○ ○ ○
116. ○ ○ ○
117. ○ ○ ○
118. ○ ○ ○
119. ○ ○ ○
120. ○ ○ ○
121. ○ ○ ○
122. ○ ○ ○
123. ○ ○ ○
124. ○ ○ ○
125. ○ ○ ○
126. ○ ○ ○
127. ○ ○ ○
128. ○ ○ ○
129. ○ ○ ○
130. ○ ○ ○
141. ○ ○ ○
132. ○ ○ ○
133. ○ ○ ○
134. ○ ○ ○

Yes ? No

135. ○ ○ ○
136. ○ ○ ○
137. ○ ○ ○
138. ○ ○ ○
139. ○ ○ ○
140. ○ ○ ○
141. ○ ○ ○
142. ○ ○ ○
143. ○ ○ ○
144. ○ ○ ○
145. ○ ○ ○
146. ○ ○ ○
147. ○ ○ ○
148. ○ ○ ○
149. ○ ○ ○
150. ○ ○ ○
151. ○ ○ ○
152. ○ ○ ○

(1) (2) (3)

153. ○ ○ ○
154. ○ ○ ○
155. ○ ○ ○
156. ○ ○ ○
157. ○ ○ ○
158. ○ ○ ○
159. ○ ○ ○
160. ○ ○ ○
161. ○ ○ ○
162. ○ ○ ○
163. ○ ○ ○
164. ○ ○ ○
165. ○ ○ ○
166. ○ ○ ○

Yes ? No

167. ○ ○ ○
168. ○ ○ ○
169. ○ ○ ○
170. ○ ○ ○
171. ○ ○ ○
172. ○ ○ ○
173. ○ ○ ○
174. ○ ○ ○
175. ○ ○ ○
176. ○ ○ ○
177. ○ ○ ○
178. ○ ○ ○
179. ○ ○ ○
180. ○ ○ ○
181. ○ ○ ○
182. ○ ○ ○
183. ○ ○ ○
184. ○ ○ ○
185. ○ ○ ○
186. ○ ○ ○
187. ○ ○ ○
188. ○ ○ ○
189. ○ ○ ○
190. ○ ○ ○
191. ○ ○ ○
192. ○ ○ ○
193. ○ ○ ○
194. ○ ○ ○
195. ○ ○ ○
196. ○ ○ ○
197. ○ ○ ○
198. ○ ○ ○
199. ○ ○ ○
200. ○ ○ ○

Yes ? No

201. ○ ○ ○
202. ○ ○ ○
203. ○ ○ ○
204. ○ ○ ○
205. ○ ○ ○
206. ○ ○ ○
207. ○ ○ ○
208. ○ ○ ○

A
B
C
D
E
F

ANSWER SHEET

Name ______________________ Date ______________________

	Yes	?	No
1.	○	○	○
2.	○	○	○
3.	○	○	○
4.	○	○	○
5.	○	○	○
6.	○	○	○
7.	○	○	○
8.	○	○	○
9.	○	○	○
10.	○	○	○
11.	○	○	○
12.	○	○	○
13.	○	○	○
14.	○	○	○
15.	○	○	○
16.	○	○	○
17.	○	○	○
18.	○	○	○
19.	○	○	○
20.	○	○	○
21.	○	○	○
22.	○	○	○
23.	○	○	○
24.	○	○	○
25.	○	○	○
26.	○	○	○
27.	○	○	○
28.	○	○	○
29.	○	○	○
30.	○	○	○
31.	○	○	○
32.	○	○	○
33.	○	○	○
34.	○	○	○

	Yes	?	No
35.	○	○	○
36.	○	○	○
37.	○	○	○
38.	○	○	○
39.	○	○	○
40.	○	○	○
41.	○	○	○
42.	○	○	○
43.	○	○	○
44.	○	○	○
45.	○	○	○
46.	○	○	○
47.	○	○	○
48.	○	○	○
49.	○	○	○
50.	○	○	○

	(1)	(2)	(3)
51.	○	○	○
52.	○	○	○
53.	○	○	○
54.	○	○	○
55.	○	○	○
56.	○	○	○
57.	○	○	○
58.	○	○	○
59.	○	○	○
60.	○	○	○
61	○	○	○
62.	○	○	○
63.	○	○	○

	Yes	?	No
64.	○	○	○
65.	○	○	○
66.	○	○	○

	Yes	?	No
67.	○	○	○
68.	○	○	○
69.	○	○	○
70.	○	○	○
71.	○	○	○
72.	○	○	○
73.	○	○	○
74.	○	○	○
75.	○	○	○
76.	○	○	○
77.	○	○	○
78.	○	○	○
79.	○	○	○
80.	○	○	○
81.	○	○	○
82.	○	○	○
83.	○	○	○
84.	○	○	○
85.	○	○	○
86.	○	○	○
87.	○	○	○
88.	○	○	○
89.	○	○	○
90.	○	○	○
91.	○	○	○
92.	○	○	○
93.	○	○	○
94.	○	○	○
95.	○	○	○
96.	○	○	○
97.	○	○	○
98.	○	○	○
99.	○	○	○

	Yes	?	No
100.	○	○	○
101.	○	○	○
102.	○	○	○
103.	○	○	○
104.	○	○	○
105.	○	○	○
106.	○	○	○
107.	○	○	○
108.	○	○	○
109.	○	○	○
110.	○	○	○
111.	○	○	○
112.	○	○	○
113.	○	○	○
114.	○	○	○
115.	○	○	○
116.	○	○	○
117.	○	○	○
118.	○	○	○
119.	○	○	○
120.	○	○	○
121.	○	○	○
122.	○	○	○
123.	○	○	○
124.	○	○	○
125.	○	○	○
126.	○	○	○
127.	○	○	○
128.	○	○	○
129.	○	○	○
130.	○	○	○
141.	○	○	○
132.	○	○	○
133.	○	○	○
134.	○	○	○

	Yes	?	No
135.	○	○	○
136	○	○	○
137.	○	○	○
138.	○	○	○
139.	○	○	○
140.	○	○	○
141.	○	○	○
142.	○	○	○
143.	○	○	○
144.	○	○	○
145.	○	○	○
146.	○	○	○
147.	○	○	○
148.	○	○	○
149.	○	○	○
150.	○	○	○
151.	○	○	○
152.	○	○	○

	(1)	(2)	(3)
153.	○	○	○
154.	○	○	○
166.	○	○	○
156.	○	○	○
157.	○	○	○
158.	○	○	○
159.	○	○	○
160.	○	○	○
161.	○	○	○
162.	○	○	○
163.	○	○	○
164.	○	○	○
165.	○	○	○
166.	○	○	○

	Yes	?	No
167.	○	○	○
168.	○	○	○
169.	○	○	○
170.	○	○	○
171.	○	○	○
172.	○	○	○
173.	○	○	○
174.	○	○	○
175.	○	○	○
176.	○	○	○
177.	○	○	○
178.	○	○	○
179.	○	○	○
180.	○	○	○
181.	○	○	○
182.	○	○	○
183.	○	○	○
184.	○	○	○
185.	○	○	○
186.	○	○	○
187.	○	○	○
188.	○	○	○
189.	○	○	○
190.	○	○	○
191.	○	○	○
192.	○	○	○
193.	○	○	○
194.	○	○	○
195.	○	○	○
196.	○	○	○
197.	○	○	○
198.	○	○	○
199.	○	○	○
200.	○	○	○

	Yes	?	No
201.	○	○	○
202.	○	○	○
203.	○	○	○
204.	○	○	○
205.	○	○	○
206.	○	○	○
207.	○	○	○
208.	○	○	○

A
B
C
D
E
F

ANSWER SHEET

Name ______________________ Date ______________________

	Yes	?	No
1.–34.			

	Yes	?	No
35.–50.			

	(1)	(2)	(3)
51.–63.			

	Yes	?	No
64.–66.			

	Yes	?	No
67.–99.			

	Yes	?	No
100.–134.			

	Yes	?	No
135.–152.			

	(1)	(2)	(3)
153.–166.			

	Yes	?	No
167.–200.			

	Yes	?	No
201.–208.			

A
B
C
D
E
F

ANSWER SHEET

Name ______________________ Date ______________________

Yes ? No

1. ○ ○ ○
2. ○ ○ ○
3. ○ ○ ○
4. ○ ○ ○
5. ○ ○ ○
6. ○ ○ ○
7. ○ ○ ○
8. ○ ○ ○
9. ○ ○ ○
10. ○ ○ ○
11. ○ ○ ○
12. ○ ○ ○
13. ○ ○ ○
14. ○ ○ ○
15. ○ ○ ○
16. ○ ○ ○
17. ○ ○ ○
18. ○ ○ ○
19. ○ ○ ○
20. ○ ○ ○
21. ○ ○ ○
22. ○ ○ ○
23. ○ ○ ○
24. ○ ○ ○
25. ○ ○ ○
26. ○ ○ ○
27. ○ ○ ○
28. ○ ○ ○
29. ○ ○ ○
30. ○ ○ ○
31. ○ ○ ○
32. ○ ○ ○
33. ○ ○ ○
34. ○ ○ ○

Yes ? No

35. ○ ○ ○
36. ○ ○ ○
37. ○ ○ ○
38. ○ ○ ○
39. ○ ○ ○
40. ○ ○ ○
41. ○ ○ ○
42. ○ ○ ○
43. ○ ○ ○
44. ○ ○ ○
45. ○ ○ ○
46. ○ ○ ○
47. ○ ○ ○
48. ○ ○ ○
49. ○ ○ ○
50. ○ ○ ○

(1) (2) (3)

51. ○ ○ ○
52. ○ ○ ○
53. ○ ○ ○
54. ○ ○ ○
55. ○ ○ ○
56. ○ ○ ○
57. ○ ○ ○
58. ○ ○ ○
59. ○ ○ ○
60. ○ ○ ○
61. ○ ○ ○
62. ○ ○ ○
63. ○ ○ ○

Yes ? No

64. ○ ○ ○
65. ○ ○ ○
66. ○ ○ ○

Yes ? No

67. ○ ○ ○
68. ○ ○ ○
69. ○ ○ ○
70. ○ ○ ○
71. ○ ○ ○
72. ○ ○ ○
73. ○ ○ ○
74. ○ ○ ○
75. ○ ○ ○
76. ○ ○ ○
77. ○ ○ ○
78. ○ ○ ○
79. ○ ○ ○
80. ○ ○ ○
81. ○ ○ ○
82. ○ ○ ○
83. ○ ○ ○
84. ○ ○ ○
85. ○ ○ ○
86. ○ ○ ○
87. ○ ○ ○
88. ○ ○ ○
89. ○ ○ ○
90. ○ ○ ○
91. ○ ○ ○
92. ○ ○ ○
93. ○ ○ ○
94. ○ ○ ○
95. ○ ○ ○
96. ○ ○ ○
97. ○ ○ ○
98. ○ ○ ○
99. ○ ○ ○

Yes ? No

100. ○ ○ ○
101. ○ ○ ○
102. ○ ○ ○
103. ○ ○ ○
104. ○ ○ ○
105. ○ ○ ○
106. ○ ○ ○
107. ○ ○ ○
108. ○ ○ ○
109. ○ ○ ○
110. ○ ○ ○
111. ○ ○ ○
112. ○ ○ ○
113. ○ ○ ○
114. ○ ○ ○
115. ○ ○ ○
116. ○ ○ ○
117. ○ ○ ○
118. ○ ○ ○
119. ○ ○ ○
120. ○ ○ ○
121. ○ ○ ○
122. ○ ○ ○
123. ○ ○ ○
124. ○ ○ ○
125. ○ ○ ○
126. ○ ○ ○
127. ○ ○ ○
128. ○ ○ ○
129. ○ ○ ○
130. ○ ○ ○
141. ○ ○ ○
132. ○ ○ ○
133. ○ ○ ○
134. ○ ○ ○

Yes ? No

135. ○ ○ ○
136. ○ ○ ○
137. ○ ○ ○
138. ○ ○ ○
139. ○ ○ ○
140. ○ ○ ○
141. ○ ○ ○
142. ○ ○ ○
143. ○ ○ ○
144. ○ ○ ○
145. ○ ○ ○
146. ○ ○ ○
147. ○ ○ ○
148. ○ ○ ○
149. ○ ○ ○
150. ○ ○ ○
151. ○ ○ ○
152. ○ ○ ○

(1) (2) (3)

153. ○ ○ ○
154. ○ ○ ○
155. ○ ○ ○
156. ○ ○ ○
157. ○ ○ ○
158. ○ ○ ○
159. ○ ○ ○
160. ○ ○ ○
161. ○ ○ ○
162. ○ ○ ○
163. ○ ○ ○
164. ○ ○ ○
165. ○ ○ ○
166. ○ ○ ○

Yes ? No

167. ○ ○ ○
168. ○ ○ ○
169. ○ ○ ○
170. ○ ○ ○
171. ○ ○ ○
172. ○ ○ ○
173. ○ ○ ○
174. ○ ○ ○
175. ○ ○ ○
176. ○ ○ ○
177. ○ ○ ○
170. ○ ○ ○
179. ○ ○ ○
180. ○ ○ ○
181. ○ ○ ○
182. ○ ○ ○
183. ○ ○ ○
184. ○ ○ ○
185. ○ ○ ○
186. ○ ○ ○
187. ○ ○ ○
188. ○ ○ ○
189. ○ ○ ○
190. ○ ○ ○
191. ○ ○ ○
192. ○ ○ ○
193. ○ ○ ○
194. ○ ○ ○
195. ○ ○ ○
196. ○ ○ ○
197. ○ ○ ○
198. ○ ○ ○
199. ○ ○ ○
200. ○ ○ ○

Yes ? No

201. ○ ○ ○
202. ○ ○ ○
203. ○ ○ ○
204. ○ ○ ○
205. ○ ○ ○
206. ○ ○ ○
20 . ○ ○ ○
208. ○ ○ ○

A
B
C
D
E
F

ANSWER SHEET

Name ______________________ Date ______________________

Yes ? No

1. ○ ○ ○
2. ○ ○ ○
3. ○ ○ ○
4. ○ ○ ○
5. ○ ○ ○
6. ○ ○ ○
7. ○ ○ ○
8. ○ ○ ○
9. ○ ○ ○
10. ○ ○ ○
11. ○ ○ ○
12. ○ ○ ○
13. ○ ○ ○
14. ○ ○ ○
15. ○ ○ ○
16. ○ ○ ○
17. ○ ○ ○
18. ○ ○ ○
19. ○ ○ ○
20. ○ ○ ○
21. ○ ○ ○
22. ○ ○ ○
23. ○ ○ ○
24. ○ ○ ○
25. ○ ○ ○
26. ○ ○ ○
27. ○ ○ ○
28. ○ ○ ○
29. ○ ○ ○
30. ○ ○ ○
31. ○ ○ ○
32. ○ ○ ○
33. ○ ○ ○
34. ○ ○ ○

Yes ? No

35. ○ ○ ○
36. ○ ○ ○
37. ○ ○ ○
38. ○ ○ ○
39. ○ ○ ○
40. ○ ○ ○
41. ○ ○ ○
42. ○ ○ ○
43. ○ ○ ○
44. ○ ○ ○
45. ○ ○ ○
46. ○ ○ ○
47. ○ ○ ○
48. ○ ○ ○
49. ○ ○ ○
50. ○ ○ ○

(1) (2) (3)

51. ○ ○ ○
52. ○ ○ ○
53. ○ ○ ○
54. ○ ○ ○
55. ○ ○ ○
56. ○ ○ ○
57. ○ ○ ○
58. ○ ○ ○
59. ○ ○ ○
60. ○ ○ ○
61. ○ ○ ○
62. ○ ○ ○
63. ○ ○ ○

Yes ? No

64. ○ ○ ○
65. ○ ○ ○
66. ○ ○ ○

Yes ? No

67. ○ ○ ○
68. ○ ○ ○
69. ○ ○ ○
70. ○ ○ ○
71. ○ ○ ○
72. ○ ○ ○
73. ○ ○ ○
74. ○ ○ ○
75. ○ ○ ○
76. ○ ○ ○
77. ○ ○ ○
78. ○ ○ ○
79. ○ ○ ○
80. ○ ○ ○
81. ○ ○ ○
82. ○ ○ ○
83. ○ ○ ○
84. ○ ○ ○
85. ○ ○ ○
86. ○ ○ ○
87. ○ ○ ○
88. ○ ○ ○
89. ○ ○ ○
90. ○ ○ ○
91. ○ ○ ○
92. ○ ○ ○
93. ○ ○ ○
94. ○ ○ ○
95. ○ ○ ○
96. ○ ○ ○
97. ○ ○ ○
98. ○ ○ ○
99. ○ ○ ○

Yes ? No

100. ○ ○ ○
101. ○ ○ ○
102. ○ ○ ○
103. ○ ○ ○
104. ○ ○ ○
105. ○ ○ ○
106. ○ ○ ○
107. ○ ○ ○
108. ○ ○ ○
109. ○ ○ ○
110. ○ ○ ○
111. ○ ○ ○
112. ○ ○ ○
113. ○ ○ ○
114. ○ ○ ○
115. ○ ○ ○
116. ○ ○ ○
117. ○ ○ ○
118. ○ ○ ○
119. ○ ○ ○
120. ○ ○ ○
121. ○ ○ ○
122. ○ ○ ○
123. ○ ○ ○
124. ○ ○ ○
125. ○ ○ ○
126. ○ ○ ○
127. ○ ○ ○
128. ○ ○ ○
129. ○ ○ ○
130. ○ ○ ○
141. ○ ○ ○
132. ○ ○ ○
133. ○ ○ ○
134. ○ ○ ○

Yes ? No

135. ○ ○ ○
136. ○ ○ ○
137. ○ ○ ○
138. ○ ○ ○
139. ○ ○ ○
140. ○ ○ ○
141. ○ ○ ○
142. ○ ○ ○
143. ○ ○ ○
144. ○ ○ ○
145. ○ ○ ○
146. ○ ○ ○
147. ○ ○ ○
148. ○ ○ ○
149. ○ ○ ○
150. ○ ○ ○
151. ○ ○ ○
152. ○ ○ ○

(1) (2) (3)

153. ○ ○ ○
154. ○ ○ ○
155. ○ ○ ○
156. ○ ○ ○
157. ○ ○ ○
158. ○ ○ ○
159. ○ ○ ○
160. ○ ○ ○
161. ○ ○ ○
162. ○ ○ ○
163. ○ ○ ○
164. ○ ○ ○
165. ○ ○ ○
166. ○ ○ ○

Yes ? No

167. ○ ○ ○
168. ○ ○ ○
169. ○ ○ ○
170. ○ ○ ○
171. ○ ○ ○
172. ○ ○ ○
173. ○ ○ ○
174. ○ ○ ○
175. ○ ○ ○
176. ○ ○ ○
177. ○ ○ ○
178. ○ ○ ○
179. ○ ○ ○
180. ○ ○ ○
181. ○ ○ ○
182. ○ ○ ○
183. ○ ○ ○
184. ○ ○ ○
185. ○ ○ ○
186. ○ ○ ○
187. ○ ○ ○
188. ○ ○ ○
189. ○ ○ ○
190. ○ ○ ○
191. ○ ○ ○
192. ○ ○ ○
193. ○ ○ ○
194. ○ ○ ○
195. ○ ○ ○
196. ○ ○ ○
197. ○ ○ ○
198. ○ ○ ○
199. ○ ○ ○
200. ○ ○ ○

Yes ? No

201. ○ ○ ○
202. ○ ○ ○
203. ○ ○ ○
204. ○ ○ ○
205. ○ ○ ○
206. ○ ○ ○
207. ○ ○ ○
208. ○ ○ ○

A
B
C
D
E
F